Rebirth within my
Heart

Sezin Aksoy

BALBOA.
PRESS

A DIVISION OF HAY HOUSE

Balboa Press books may be ordered through booksellers or by contacting:

Balboa Press
A Division of Hay House
1663 Liberty Drive
Bloomington, IN 47403
www.balboapress.com
1 (877) 407-4847

Printed in the United States of America.

ISBN: 978-1-4525-2189-3 (sc)
ISBN: 978-1-4525-2190-9 (e)

Balboa Press rev. date: 09/08/2014

This book is dedicated to my mother,
Nilgul Aksoy, who has always been there for me...

Introduction

I believe 'Heart is the center of the body.' But some believe that belly is. Well after having a dramatic but a wonderful growth lesson with my heart, I made my choice about my center. In my opinion, how I treated my heart responded to my life so that it should have been my center. I was lucky that I met the right people at the right time during my time of healing. My prayers, my belief and my strength helped me to meet the best opportunities at the best time. It is called Divine Timing for me but some could call this, wonderful coincidences of life or miracles.

My story that I share here is the healing process I went through before and after my heart surgery. I believe that I was prepared to have the surgery, the growth lesson given to me, couple of years before. There are lots of chains of activities that lead me to the process. All the experiences that I went through thought me a lesson on how to be strong, faithful, positive and loving. I learned to look at life from a different view. I understood what they meant by choosing to look at the full side of the glass of water. Gratitude, hope and grace always filled my glass. Patience was my best medicine and still is. I should have been a good student that God rewarded me with my life and chose not to take it away from me.

I experienced a difficult time but never chose to complain but only watch my process and choosing to learn from all. I always did my best to be kind and loving to everyone around me even in my worst conditions of pain. My positive attitude led others and me to happiness. I felt like God held my hand through the process by letting me come across great people who supported or directed me. I called those people angels in disguise sent by God, messengers or thought adjusters. I met the right doctors, friends, teachers, lover, therapists, psychologist, tarot readers, fitness coach, trainer, and many other valuable people. I did not just come across these people, whom were just there in my need; life leaded me to find them. Even in my own solitude, I was never alone. I saw 'the signs' in the books that I read, views that I looked, speeches that I heard and thoughts that I heard in my mind.

It led me to the question; 'What is the difference between coincidence, opportunity, destiny and faith?' As I time travel in my past today, I can build the links. Than I just thank God for helping me to grow and always showing me the way. I can never know how things would be possible without faith. No matter which answer I chose, the strength inside me always stood beside me. All that I experienced lead me to an answer. Today I see no difference between a coincidence, opportunity, faith, and even destiny but only accepting things as beautiful as they are. All the coincidences were my opportunity and at the end my destiny showed me the faith. I learned to believe in the unity of the ways. All that mattered was Divine Timing.

My journey;

Began by meeting the right therapist, Dr. Şule Tokmakçıoğlu, who thought me the way to meditate on my heart chakra, use positive affirmations, and more in the year 2007. Five years of dedication and search on my self has charged my batteries and given my soul strength. My doctor led me to the right books, spiritual teachings, and sources to find my self or I should say my life purpose. She has thought me to find the light and I chose to follow. Afterwards, I heard the little voice within me and it grew stronger with every experience in every each day. It is the voice of my heart and my soul. The voice showed me the way to set myself free and also create my own borders. Then, I had the chance to meet the right people, places and opportunities. I found my life purpose, self-encouragement, belief system and my own spiritual path. I am always thankful to her for her share of knowledge. I am grateful to God to let me find her. She thought me many things but most important was Dr. Şule Tokmakçıoğlu's efforts to show me how to analyze myself and then choose the right affirmations to heal my found situation.

First I would like to share with you the overall affirmations I said to myself during my healing process after my surgery. I had the chance to gather them all after a long meditation. Later I took the marker to write all those lines on the canvas before I started to paint my painting called 'My elevating heart within light' on the cover of this book.

My Heart Chakra Affirmations:

I ask for Divine Love and Light to lead me – my actions, my thoughts and my way of living. I am healed, whole, well and blessed. All is well, loved and reasonable. All has a reason, a meaning, a teaching for growth. Be grateful, patient and aware of All…

I let go. Choose peace for my well being. Letting me the freedom to be me. Free of charge and control. Accepting who 'I am' for whomever 'I is'… Opening my self to Endless Opportunities. Infinite way of Life. Wisdom of true living in All.

I surrender. Let go of power or control issues… Let it Be. No more dilemma or drama. Choose happiness for my Highest good. I Let Love over Fear. Releasing my judgments, what-to-be or what-not-to-be hierarchies. So Be it…

Love is me. I am loved, loving and lovefull. All is love. I let love to guide me. Being love hearted in my veins for my self and surroundings… All is one, united and whole. Consciousness of unity comes from 'love of Self'. Be to Be.

Stay in Peace by Being in your Presence. Now is my reality. Present moment is my only awareness. Stay at the moment. Clear your thoughts. Focus on your only reality, presence, moment; which is your Breathing…

Connecting with my Higher Self. Love is all around me. I breathe in love. Breathe out fear. I accept All within and around me. I forgive. Thankful of my being, presence and self… I choose love over self-hatred. Just Breathe…

Healing is in and around me. Breathing All within me. Leaving all outer illusion to itself. My presence is my wealth. I am surrounded with abundance, healing love and light, awareness and wisdom. Joy is surrounding me. I am connected…

I live in harmony of Divine Reality with Trust and Faith. All is good as I trust in self. Listening to high frequencies of Light. My heart elevates with love and light. Breathing in light directly to my heart. Opening my heart to All in trust…

Whole in presence of Now. Lost and found within my own peace. Grounded to earth as I travel. I am conscious, blank but nothing over something as I slide within my space of eternal Light. Now is All. All is Light. Infinity…

Now I realize, there is no right but only bright heart. No truth but only well-being of oneness. No kindness but choice of being good hearted in presented life. None of the rules apply to the heart but only listening to inner wisdom.

Pure in choice. Clear of thoughts. Blank in attitude towards life. Pain is strength. Hardship brings gratitude. So all is well at the end. Choice is towards aligning Self into new level of being. Change is imminent. Accept in peace…

Balance in giving and receiving. All is in balance and harmony. Loving self unconditionally. Opening heart to greater love by self-respect and value. Unlimited source gives in trust and receives unconditionally. As you give as you receive…

Whatever goes whatever comes. All is innocent and pure. All is rewarded. No expectancies. Divine Timing rewards all actions in loving attitude. Whatever goes comes around. Just be aware and in peace. Believe in Higher Self.

Time is an illusion in the search of spirit to learn, to grow and to love. Home is where your heart is. Return home. Love is the key to your home. Keep your home clean. Clear your heart. Clean your soul. Cut the cord…

Be independent. Free. Light-hearted. Be good. Be happy. Be selfless. I am all that I am. Shifting my awareness between these lines. Visiting Parallel Universes in my own reality. Endless source of creative energy goes through me.

Everything happens for my highest good and I will find abundance, wealth and human love in my life. Harmony and quietness is in and around me. I am blessing my thoughts, my actions and my life. Grace is my path.

Compassion is my choice. Empathy to All is my salvation. I welcome the differences within and around me. It is my nature to love. My heart is full, whole and loving. I see evidence of love all around me. I give and receive love freely.

Joy fills every vein of my heart, cell in my body. Every cell is alive with love and light. Comfort moves through me now and always. I relax into the healing process of light. I am healed, loved and whole. All is me.

I trust in faith. I am doing the best that I can in Love. Let go of all that I know. Have courage to move on… Leaving the darkness behind. Leaving the past behind. Accepting change with blessing and gratitude.

I nurture my inner-child. I will be gentle with my self. I am gentle to my self. I am tender to my heart. I am easy on my self. I love my self like a loving child. I will be tender to my heart. Nurture my heart.

I choose hope. I am hope. Hope anchors my soul. I let go in trust, peace and only love. I forgive my self. Forgive times that I forgot me. Love sets me free. There is only love in and around me. My heart is full.

I am patience. Patience is my acceptance. Surrender and let go in peace. Believe in self-empowerment. I am responsible of me, my choices, actions and thoughts. Be responsible of relations with self. Creator of my choices.

All is valuable. Everything is me. I am nothing. I am good and evil. Choice is mine, my responsibility. Rest is illusion. I am Me. I am You. All is me. All leads to the veins of the heart. Creation starts within.

All is Love. Love is All. Love lives in All. Believe and trust in All. I ask for Divine Love and Light to be with me now and always. I and All is same and everywhere. I look within to see All…

Once I find me, I find All as Eternity. Love for eternity. Love for me. Love is the path of me. Path to nothing. Love in Parallel Universes of Eternity. I am the path of love, secret of infinity. Way of soul…

Come as you are. Come just to come to love. Come as good or as evil but just come as you are to love. Whoever or whatever comes to my heart. Come once or twice as you want. Just come as you are to the heart. To my heart just come.

I am coming home. And I am coming home. My beloved, kindness of heart, breath of Life. I am about to come… And I am coming home. I choose my path to coming home. Divine Teacher, Beloved Friend sitting behind time and space…

This is my way. Kindness of the heart leads to the soul. This is your way… Let us meditate on the light of the sun which represents God, and may our thoughts be inspired by that Divine light – Gayatri Mantra…

Mantra for the heart: Ra Ma Das Sa Sa Say So Hung: "The Service of God is Within me. I am Thou" – Healing and protection to All within and around me. Thanks to All. I thank you and me. All is one.

CHAPTER I

Monday, November 19, 2012

Mondays are the beginning of the week. Beginning of work or school and for some leisure. I have always seen it, as the beginning of week like most people do but Monday November 19 was the day for me to wake up early and get ready to go to hospital. It was the day before my heart surgery. Also it is the date of my ex-boyfriend's birthday, my first love, whom that I have not talked for months after the breakup and also never said a word for one year even if he heard about my surgery. This Monday was the true beginning for me. I would say it was the day before my rebirth or could call heart cleanse.

I had trouble with Mondays as long as I had trouble at school. I had a rough childhood. My teacher at primary school was a middle-aged woman with dried red hair and red fur coat who always smelled almonds. She was always frustrated, unhappy or angry with her students. I was only six years old when I met her at my first day of school. She looked complicated and full of authority. I was afraid of her stare into my eyes that asked me to keep my silence. She was hard to be pleased but all day standing beside me. So when I had my mother's warmth at home during the weekends, it was very difficult to leave the house on Mondays and head for school to meet my teacher. I had nightmares of my primary school teacher watching over me at nights. Unfortunately I had to meet her in real time every morning of the week for three years. It was stressful. Twenty-five years later, I felt the same pain in my stomach when I left my house for the hospital. I felt like I was heading to school. I was walking towards somewhere that I did not want to go but had no other choice other than going.

I packed all my cloths that I needed. Most importantly I packed my crystals, icons, Mother Mary statue and Ganesh, unicorn, happy Buddha, and most importantly I wore my little gold pray which my father bought for me to save me during my surgery. I put them in my pink bag with flowers, put on my kitty cat sweater for luck. I looked around to feel the warmth of my house. It was all white, bright, big and sweet. The air in my room was fresh from the forest outside. I was always feeling small in my parent's house. It was not because it was a big house. It was because it reminded me my childhood and had my parents' warmth.

My Parents House

My mother and father live right next to a forest. It is a tree-floored house and my room is on the basement looking at the garden and the pool. It is very peaceful with a pleasant view of the trees and flowers. My mother likes to spend time in her garden planting her flowers or having tea under her magnolia tree. I always like to join her during summers when I give a break between my paintings. The peaceful atmosphere of the house is always healing to me. My small Yorkshire terrier walks elegantly in the house as if she is the daughter of the house. My father likes to read his paper in front of the fireplace during the cold winter nights. It is always warm in my house whether it is winter or summer. I call it the charm of family weather.

I was told to take things easy and watch out for my self before my surgery. So the house smelled fresh cooked bakery or meal every day during that week. Everyone was worried but nobody was allowed to show or talk about it. The reason was that I should not get afraid and sensed the importance of the event coming up. Our neighbors came for visits. They stayed for dinners and coffee so that they would bring in different conversations. We were so lucky that we had good neighbors that were there for us when we needed. Unfortunately, it is so hard to find good neighbors in cosmopolitan cities these days. We are blesses in that sense that we built good relations with them. I was lazy and tired all the time. Probably I had too much going on my mind that I was trying to push behind. So I was multi tasking every moment. Thinking of the event coming up and also trying to eat, talk or make conversations was too difficult for me. I was fighting with myself to quiten my mind, which was the simplest task for me before. There was huge silence in the house after our visitors left so that the long serious conversations were kept in the eyes of the real occupants of the house.

Life Review

As long as I was moving to a new apartment and had no place to stay and needed some special care and assistance, I moved to my parents' house a week before the nineteenth eleven twelve. That one-week was a silent treat for me. I was processing and evaluating the end of my relationships, move from my first apartment, the close end of year two thousand twelve, the lucky dragon year. I was thinking of how the year 2012 passed for me and how my years before prepared me to that year. I was questioning my life, my decisions, my reasons, my friends, my lovers, my social life and most importantly health.

I came to a conclusion that it was really my lucky year. When I thought of my health, I did not only evaluate my physical health but also my emotional, psychic and psychological health, which might have caused my body to react through this illness. As long as I had this problem since birth or childhood than I should have review it all since the beginning. I knew that it would have been difficult but I had so much time ahead of me that I needed to in order to get healthy in full pack. Fear would not take me to a conclusion but only focus. I should have face my self in order to receive my reward. I finally understood that our life mission was to pass the tests with the self. In that sense, I could not achieve my score by complaining, wining or crying but only finding my own solution and cure.

I asked for God to assist me and angels to show me the light during this challenge. Only God would show me the way and the angels would only be there to protect me. I prayed every night before sleep. I asked my angels to enter my dreams so that I could understand the depth of my thinking. I asked them to calm my thoughts so that I could follow them easier. I wanted them to ease my pain so that I would not feel my physical pains when they would come. I was the only one who would be there for myself. God was my only protector. I was the only presence in my own reality. The rest including my family and friends were there for me sent by God and my angels. So I thanked Divine presence first and than the angels in disguise. I tried to see everyday how lucky I was. Whatever was happening it was only happening for my own good. They were all there for my growth. So I was ready to review my life...

When I came to the point of evaluating my physical health, I was thinking of the days that I was generally tired, breathless and weak. I was always understood as a person that was out of sport games and activities with long walks, running or even too warm places. I chose to be unsocial to protect myself. I was always challenged by my parents and teachers to face the people around me by going out there to attend the activities. I tried but when I realized that I could not, I just gave up. So I always felt guilty that I could not succeed my challenges that my self-esteem went down. I learned to be a loner. It was good in a sense that I created my own world. I made my imaginary friends. I chose to draw. I was also lucky that my mother was so good to me at home. I was always out of the games as long as I was not able to run but it was fine. I got used to it.

Running was my big dream. I dreamed of running like a tiger but never did even if I tried every kind of sport and exercise. I did not know the reason behind it nor did my parents. My mother took me to doctors but they labeled me as a fragile. We always thought it was the way of me. I was probably a naive person, which I never wanted to accept. I wanted to be though and strong like my other friends so that I would be in the group. Children were cruel as well. When they saw a fragile, they named her a sissy. Well if I was a sissy than I was. I remember watching people playing sports and I was only left to hate the ball. I hated it because I was never able to run behind it and able to catch it. Before I was there my breathing would stop me. When I forced it, I would faint. When I fainted than my teachers would be in panic. Than I would explain them my situation and they would tell me that I should eat more. Well I turned out to be a chubby. So I was always out of the games. I was a chubby penguin as long as I was walking abnormal because of my flat feet. Well what could I do? My lovely mother told me to stand up for myself. My lovely father told me to see the humor in it. So I did. I smiled when people laughed at me. I asked them to mind their own business. I desolated myself every each day. The good thing was that I was not able to see the reason behind it all at that time but it all changed today.

Now, I was only imagining a neon tiger running beside me after my renewal. I was only hoping. So I dreamed of myself running every night before the surgery.

Evaluation process

I kept thinking of the shape of my heart tumor, myxoma, which had been with me since birth. I was wondering if it was big or small. How it would be removed? Should I ask more about the process? Should I ask or just let it be? What if something would go wrong? Would I survive or not? Was my heart strong enough? Would I be strong enough after the surgery? How would my life be after the surgery? Would it hurt? Will the neon tiger show up? I would stop... Other questions about my life would storm in.

As I placed thought on my relationships and myself through evaluating it with the coming up surgery I realized so many truths that I chose to ignore. I thought about how much time and energy I placed up on my relationships before myself. I realized how I forgot the self-respect and love that I needed to place on me. However, life was short and very important while I was busy with others needs and ego-issues. I had placed so little time thinking of my needs. It was wonderful to be selfless but it was good when it was done in a proper manner. I needed to learn to build healthy boundaries. Self-respect was not about being cruel or unkind but when done in a proper manner and joy than it would bring prosperity to relationships. Borders should only be there to reflect the love and respect you choose to have for your self, the rest would be a show up. Kindness and tenderness was so important but first had to be around for my self than for others. I learned this through the process of understanding the meaning of relationships and later finding the hierarchy in them.

The most important relationship is the relation with God and than the self, later with family that always reflects you perfectly, afterwards intimate ones such as lovers, friends, teachers, partners or co-workers that you meet everyday and lastly acquaintances you see around. The relation that you made with yourself is always reflected onto others. The relation with God and the self is very important and the rest are the tools that are sent by God in order for you to face your self. As they come, as they go, you grow on if you dare to see yourself onto others... Think of them as raindrops and your self as a tree reaching up as the drops are passing by in order for you to grow. Some drops are fall unto you and some passes you but they are all sent from above.

God is the most important relationship in a way to build trust and belief within the self. God is viewed differently for every each person. I always chose to believe in my own view of God who is there for me to protect and guide me. God is there to give me the challenges and rewards. I called God as 'All' because God is the presence in all and also absence in everything. God is the Father as a protector and Mother as a life giver. God lives in different poles, sexes and polarities so we should love both as long as we love God. All is in unity, peace and love. I felt peaceful and protected in this kind of belief system that I built for my self since my childhood. I don't remember anyone teaching me this but I always knew it.

I prayed God in every language, way and understanding that I learned. I chose all the tools to connect me to Divine Life Force. I respected every view as long as God is the source, the creator and healer of all. I never judged any tool or view as long as I was not there to judge but God was. Karma is there to judge. So I trust. I hope. Keep the faith. I learned to love in return. This leaded me to a perfect relationship with self. That gave me patience and eased me when I needed to let go things as they were. When I had a good relationship with the self with peace than I was able to build a better one with others. My most important relationship was with God and life alone itself. I only needed to focus on my life review, which was my most important life mission.

Through years I met people that did not believe in anything. I met with people that were not happy. I started to question them. I wanted to understand them. I also wanted to be a part of the larger group. So I chose to change. I wanted to be popular. I wanted to be loved. I wanted to be praised. I wanted to be flattered. I forgot that all was in me. I just needed others to give me what I needed to give to myself. So there was lack of love as long as I was using people around me unconsciously when I was begging for love.

School years had taken away the self-respect and love away from me. In order to be part of something, I left the part of myself. Through years I gave up praying, believing and loving. I built a false border around me. Actually I built a fence around me for protection but that hurt me in return. It was not because my sign was cancer. It was not because I was a woman. It was not because I was a painter. In conclusion, it was not because of my identity. Identity was just a game of ego. It was only because of believing the lack but not the unlimited prosperity of the source.

Now, life put a challenge over me. This was a time for me to question myself and have an overview of how much meaning I placed over my life. For ten years of therapy I learned to evaluate my self, relationships, ego, emotions and soul. I meditated on my childhood and learned how to love and have compassion for others and myself. I imagined to radiate sun over my head, cleansed my soul with pink air, so on and forth but nothing was a real waking call for me.

The short notification of a heart surgery was a strong alarm. Probably, it was given to me as a teaching after my motivation to find the way. Heart chakra meditations have asked me to focus on my heart. I thought I was doing it in a perfect manner. Though I was wrong. During that one week, I learned to really connect into my inner self in order to hear my heart by feeling its rhythm in every beat and felt its presence in my ears. I always heard the sound of my heart but this time differently because I felt its cry for help.

I was ready to be there for my heart. I was ready to go deep within me and hear the cry and need of myself. I knew that I was so valuable to give this gift to myself.

Crying Heart

This experience became a connection to my core, being and life force. It was an awakening experience to overview my emotional self. I realized I was putting so much pressure to my self by creating psychological dramas. My fears were creating all the drama scenes that were not even there at the end. I woke up from my life, which was filled with suffering. I was only unhappy because of the negativity I was causing to my self. I had times that I asked for a quick end to my life. Why? It was only because I wanted to stop all that scenarios and negative evaluations that my ego created for its own strength struggles.

When life showed me that it could easily stop than, I realized how precious my life was and how important it is to stay alive. I felt the support given to me from above and realized that I was not alone. All the solutions, the answers and the most important questions were within me. When I felt that connection with a fools trust. The support started to flow within me. My heart started to cry less. I felt its beat more meaningful. My emotional responses felt better and more meaningful. The meaning of listening to self started to appear within. Every view and opinion was also precious but only in its own carrier. So everybody walks its own path in its own wisdom. When I was ready, the meanings would appear to me. So they did. After I believed that the answers would appear to me, I started to receive emails, see articles, hear conversations between people and even meet the people that could help me. They were not just coincidences. They were there in my need.

Every person I faced started to seem like an angel in disguise. Every each place I walked in started to look different. The reason was that I had a belief in me that whatever was happening was only happening for my highest good. This was appreciating life by taking every challenge as a game by choosing to enjoy it. All I needed to do was sending my gratitude to every growth lesson. Bad times were given to me to understand how beautiful good times were. Good times were like a break from bad times to enjoy. I needed them both to learn.

November 19th 2012 was a date for me to stop joking about life and get serious to work on my life purpose, to learn to stay in peace, and become happy. It was a new chapter in my life, a time to clean dark clouds and put some light and laughter in good and bad days. So I took a brave step into my school to the hospital as every one else had seen it as.

CHAPTER II

My First Apartment no.1

After I finished college, I moved back to my country and started to live in my parents' apartment. Living alone for eight years in United States after high school, it was very hard for me to move back into my parents' place. It took me two years to adapt to their environment. My work was going slow, which was making me frustrated and more difficult to find a gallery to work with. My space was very small for my large size paintings. So I started to dream on finding an apartment to use as an artist's studio. I was trying to change my life but was not able to figure it out.

One day, I decided to make myself a dream board. I collected some photos from different kinds of magazines. I picked a photo of a studio entrance, which was very retro looking probably from the fifties. It was a white wood entrance with marble floors. I cut and pasted it onto my closet door so that I would see it every time I opened. I looked at it for couple of months with so much enthusiasm and high expectancies that afterwards

I started to feel more and more away from it. I got used to the picture and forgot about it. Couple of years later, I realized that I was beginning to loose my interest in it.

At the end, I even stopped paying attention to my dreams and became so pessimistic and unhappy that I was actually becoming lost in my fear of lack. When my parents decided to move to a new house, I decided to throw away the pictures on my dream board and just moved to their new house. In my family's new place, I had a large space to work on my own but felt not belonging to the house. I was able to work on my paintings but still longing for my own space and independence. I was not aware of what I was doing. Only lost in the hopelessness of not valuing my needs and desires.

A year later, I received a phone call from a very respectful friend of my grandparents. He wanted to tell me that he was moving out of his apartment and looking for someone to rent his space for an affordable price. He tried to convince me and explained me how good it would be for me to move into a new place and have a new beginning. It was important for a painter to be independent so that my concentration would be higher. I was so used to my parents' new place and was so afraid to move out of my comfort zone that I ignored his offer first. However, I knew that he was speaking on my behalf.

Change was a big issue for me at that time. I had a fear of change. I was taking it as a bad sign instead of seeing it as a breakthrough from old habits to open new doors for better opportunities. I was underestimating my self-value so that I never thought that Universe would offer me better chances in new occasions.

I was so lazy and laid back to make new life styles. In that manner, I kept lying to myself by telling that it would be hard to move as long as I had just moved to a new place. Just continued on coming up with useless excuses and was not aware that it was my ego speaking. Thanks God that our respectful family friend strongly insisted on me to give the apartment a chance by just checking it so that I could not say no. Therefore, we scheduled a date to meet in front of his apartment for rent.

Apartment for rent

It was a nice sunny day. I was very excited to see the apartment as soon as I found out that it was on the street where I dreamed to live since I was a child. I was feeling hopeless and also longing to have a new beginning but was not aware how to begin. It was hard for me to open up to my parents and tell them what I want. It was easier for me to sleep on things. So that I was choosing not to evaluate my needs, look for opportunities and dare to talk about them. I would rather not fight for them but wait for a miracle. However miracles were laid in front of me and were just waiting for me to realize and accept.

On the way to the meeting, I was dreaming about the place. The fear got all over me. I was so afraid to like the place so that I would need to talk it over with my parents and upset them. My parents were happy to live with me.

They thought that I would live with them as long as it would take me. It was time for me to lay my cards on the table. Even if I had a chance to rent it, I would prefer to sleep on my dreams. It was hard for me to tell them something they would not like to hear. Struggling with all those thoughts, I forgot to enjoy the moment. I was trying to convince myself that I would not like the place. Kept telling myself that I had no chance to rent the space that I should stop visualizing the apartment. It was like devils were sitting on top of my head and fighting over my angelic thoughts. On the other hand, my good thinking was still so surprised that I received an opportunity like that without even searching on it. It was something that I always wanted and it just came to me right when I needed. So a voice within me was telling me to go for it. That voice was so much like my angels' sound.

Our friend met us in front of the apartment. He was a very respected and well-known person that everybody knew him in the neighborhood. So moving to his place would be good for me as he strongly suggested. We shook hands and smiled when we arrived in front of the apartment with a rental sign on one of the windows. I was so surprised when I saw the apartment. The reason was that it was the apartment I kept pointing at when I was a child. I thought it was such a funny coincidence. The good voice inside me said it was my lucky day. Our friend presented us the building and started to give us its brief history.

It was a building constructed in fifties by an architect whose wife was a violinist. The architect was a very extra-ordinary man who was in arts and knew many painters through his time. So he built the buildings outer design depending on the authentic carpet designs of Turkey. The name of the apartment was house with kilim, which is the name of the traditional carpet of Turkey. It was fairly a small apartment with four floors with one person living on each stair. Everyone briefly knew each other that it had a cozy atmosphere. Our respectful friend's close friends were on the first floor, that he would introduce them to me later. This would help me to get familiarized with the surrounding.

His place for rent was on the entrance floor of the building. He opened the main door and pointed us the painting facing us at the entrance of the residence. It was a cubist painting of a woman figure, probably a geisha. It was in exquisite colors, which hypnotized me at the first glance. So we spent some time there enjoying the wall painting. He walked into the flat and continued on walking towards the door across the escalator on the main floor, which had a sign no1 at the door. We were following him while he was searching for his keys. Suddenly when I headed towards the door, the number on the door 1 grabbed my attention because my house number in college was eleven with two 1s. I did not know at that time the meaning hidden behind numbers but felt something exquisite behind it. Something mysterious maybe called luck. I kept my excitement quiet by just thinking that it was only a coincidence. Finally, keys were found to unlock the door to the apartment, which I would live the following three years of my life. So well how could I put this? I can say coincidences had just started in my life.

Interior design

We stepped into a room. The entrance room had old black and white marble floors and natural wood bars from fifties almost like the photo I tore from a magazine three years before. Instead of white bars, these were brown. I suddenly had goose bumps all over me. The place was too old and never been renovated since it was built but it was exceptional for me. The atmosphere of the house felt like the architect and the violinist were still there. There was a very long corridor right next to the entrance door, which was heading towards the three back rooms. The corridor was used for the violinist to study her sonatas. I thought I heard the music but was told that it was coming from up-stair neighbors, who also loved to listen to classical music every afternoon. It was like a dream come true.

One room was the living room, the second room was the bedroom, and the third room was just ideal for me to store my paintings. All the rooms had closets. One of the closets in the living room had small compartments, specially built for the violinist to put her music notes. It was left as it is since the last landlord bought the place. I fell in love. They were so old that some were broken or moved but I did not mind. The floors were painted but they were all cracked and repainted several times. The rooms had cheers in them. I was sensing the moves in them. They all looked inspiring to me. The bathrooms were like coming out of Hitchcock movie that they needed some renovation. They were so black that I was unhappy with them. However, the rent was very good and affordable that I realized I could live in it.

At the end of the week, I met with the landlord and decided to sign the contract and rent the place. I sat around with my parents and explained them the situation peacefully. They were sad that I would be moving out but accepted it. I also learned to live with the idea that not everyone would be happy with my choices. I only prayed for them to get adapted and become happy with time. They knew that I was an adult and was longing to have my own place so they understood. All turned out to be better than I thought. There was no need for drama.

So… My journey began.

Renovations

I made couple of brief changes in the apartment so it became cleaner and easier to live and work. I let the carpenters to enter the house so that they would fix the kitchen and the bathrooms. I asked them to repaint the walls. Meanwhile, I was tired and had to place to work so I took a break with my best friends. We flew to Paris for the weekend. It was the best vacation I have ever had.

As my house was getting renovated, I was also enjoying myself after a long time. It was very difficult for me to decide and take a vacation. The flights were usually so tiring for me. On the other hand, I was more a home lover than a traveller. When my best friends insisted on me to give a break, I listened to them. It was a lovely weekend.

I met new people. Actually I met a wonderful designer who became a very good friend. In the upcoming years he was the one that introduced me to lovely new people.

Paris was great with exhibitions, restaurants, streets and the language itself. It cleared my mind. We had so much fun. We went out every night and came back to our hotel room in the morning. On our last day, we visited Notre Dame de Paris. We walked in the cathedral, felt the atmosphere, lit candles and prayed. I only wished to find the true love. We prayed in front of Mother Mary statue and took beautiful photographs in order to remember the moment. I bought a charm to protect me. Later I wore it everyday. It was a beautiful Sunday and was also the day to leave. We took out flights to go back to our homes. So I went back to my new beginning.

When I came back the apartment was renewed and ready for me to move in and start working. It took me some time to adapt into the new environment. I organized the place and adapted through days. I even threw a small open studio event where I invited every person I knew so that they would learn my new place. I celebrated with everyone my new beginning. My friends, family, coworkers from the past, family friends, gallery owners, artists and many more people were invited and came for a visit. I even met my old friends that I did not get the chance to see for years.

First one year, I only used the studio as a working space so I continued on living in my parents place. The next year, I started to live in it. Once I started to live in the place, I started to feel the space more alive. There were small details of the family members traces. Forgotten stickers in the closets, some little drawings of the height measurements of the kids that lived in the house, and cracked floor paints were all there telling a story to me. I always believed that every object had a life within it with its history. So I was feeling it.

The place was strange and very lively at the same time. I felt like the house was also breathing with me. When I started to spend more time alone and adapt to the new atmosphere, I started to work extra hours. My paintings were starting to tell me a story of the place and me. I felt like something was whispering to me in the house. Maybe knowing the history of the house made it alive for me but without question I was changing.

I rented the place in November and moved into it after the new years. So I would say my journey with apartment no 1 started in the year of 2010.

CHAPTER III

Christmas

December has always been a lucky month for me. I have moved to my first apartment no.1 in December 2010. I opened my first solo exhibition in that year and the following year I met my first love of my life. In those three years my life changed enormously. I grew up mentally, emotionally and most importantly spiritually in those two years. Every kind of first was happening for me. The apartment number one was meant to be showing the firsts. I started to read so many books on self-improvements and spiritually in that year. I also started meeting or coming across like-minded people and make new friends. I was taking classes that have changed my view and also my thought process. Life started to look more differently. As an artist my work has started to modify and change. My attitude toward life shifted hundred and eighty degrees so did my circle of friends. At the end, some of my friends has left my life and some stayed with me during that process so we became closer. Overall, I realized that I was experiencing what I was reading in the books or learning through life at that time.

Every Christmas before the new years, I was making a list of wishes. I was concentrating on the list and adapting into my resolutions. The year that I moved into my apartment, I was just wishing on a new relationship, fame and success. After the new years I had a boyfriend just for two month who had encouraged and motivated me to make changes in my life. He stayed very short in my life but given me a view. I realized that he came into my life for a reason. He helped me to open my eyes and decide to live in the studio and live onto my dreams instead of deciding on what my parents asks from me. I was old enough to stand up for my beliefs. He thought me to listen to every ones views but also evaluate them depending on my own desires. So he helped me to think independently and consider on moving into my studio. In the next December, which was nearly my second year in the studio, I started to live and work in the apartment. So I was able to make more paintings. In that year, for Christmas and new years I went to Lisbon with my family, my best friend and her family.

Lisbon for Christmas

December 2010 my family and my best friends family decided to go to Lisbon for the new years time. They asked us to join them. We accepted it as long as we had no plans and wanted a change. It has been a long time since I did not travel with my family that it would be a wonderful experience.

However, it turned out to be a strange experience with the weather. It was the strangest couple of days for my friend and me. We meditated every night in the hotel room. There were huge tropical rainstorms every night that we saw them as soul cleansings. We traveled to different touristic places during the day with the family. Touristic places were for summer vacations so that most of them were closed and empty but extra ordinary and beautiful. All the houses had Christmas ornaments on them with little lights. All the balconies had small Christmas flags with Jesus paintings on them. It was beautiful.

Strangely I was looking for Mother Mary statues during the whole visit but there were only El Fatima statues. Portuguese people believed in El Fatima as Mother Mary and they were choosing to pray on El Fatima instead of Mother Mary. I could not forget the faces of the statues but could not dare to buy them as long as I wanted to find Mother Mary. On the new years night I made twelve wishes in the traditional way of Portuguese. I asked for health, peace, love, success, spiritual wisdom, a great relationship for growth and only to be with the man that I admired at that time. So I repeated his name several times. We threw confetti's, drank some champagne and danced with our family. It was a lovely night with big fireworks thrown in the center of the city. We enjoyed them and repeated our wishes with a smile on our faces.

The next day we visited a Fado place and listened to wonderful Fado singers in a traditional restaurant.

They were all very inspirational. We visited beautiful art museums and bought nice gifts for our friends. Lots of historical sight seeing were made and information was given to us by a nice tour guide. Our last day was a sunny day that we took long walk in the city of Lisbon. We enjoyed the long streets with long trees and their shades. We took many photographs. We enjoyed the moment and waved goodbye to the city. We departed back to our home.

When I came back from the travel, I met the person that I wished for in Lisbon. Actually I met him before I left for Lisbon but I met him after I came back. He was a charming nice man. We met several times and later he became a part of my life. I would say he was the first love to me because I was never attracted to someone that deeply. When we were together, I was just happy. We had great conversations together. He made me think and question my life. He thought great life lessons to me because he was a bit different than me.

He was a workaholic so was I at that time. I was not aware of it but he helped me to realize. He helped me to see the beauty in me. When he was sharing his deep secrets or personal stories, they were so similar to me that I started to question my life with him. He was so kind to me that I realized I have not been with someone nice to me for so long.

Unfortunately he changed with time. He chose to distance himself. As I was so attached to him I could not accept his distance. He tried to explain it to me several times but I was not able to accept it. I started to force things for myself with struggle. He started to act different as well. When I was letting go and giving him the distance than he was coming back to my life. It was like a war of struggles. I became so tired and restless. I should have put an end to it at that time but was not mature enough to know how.

It was a very difficult love relationship for me. His way of looking at love relationships were so different and he was so independent. I had never met somebody like him before that I did not know what to do. My friends and family were so worried for me. I became against my close friends and also family. I decided to let things find its way, which was also something totally new to me as I was a control freak. I decided it but I was not able to achieve it. As I was letting go, he was just appearing back in my life and I was so in love that I was not able to put my distance. He was so nice that I was forgetting his faults. After a year, I lost trust in him but I was so obsessed with fixing the relationship, which was not even there. We broke up and he met someone else which put an end to the relationship. I was heart broken but finally free from all the drama.

The struggle through my love life has thought me a lot during those two years. The relationship helped me to grow emotionally strong. We were so different and a part but I was trying to keep up with him in order to make us stay together. It was giving a wrong quest and struggle but learned from my mistakes. I was kind of dreaming in black clouds but at the same time trying to find the light called love in the dark. Love was a process of adaptation and change for me instead of sharing and celebrating life at that time. The process thought me what was right and wrong for me.

Everything started to be reflected on my paintings and writings as well. They were changed tremendously. When I was trying to find my path, I started to work on collages. I started to study numerology and read books on them and apply them on my work. The work was a way for me to move away from the sadness and struggle and find a path. I was kind of healing my broken heart at that time through my artwork. I wanted to share my story on that space. I let my work show me the way.

The first good part was that I dared to make mistakes and tried to push things towards the end. I made many mistakes but chose to learn through them instead of craving on repeating them. I caused too much pain to myself and the people around me by letting myself become unhappy but it improved me. The emotional pain was kind of teaching me to be strong. However, I was aware that I was so much blinded with love, which I had never been before. Therefore I became a stranger to myself as well. I was not able to understand my reactions and attitude. This kind of experience has helped me to understand myself.

The second good part was I was letting myself to break the shield that I built around myself through years. That shield was like the Chinese wall around my heart to protect me from emotional pain. So shedding that skin or shield helped me to become a different person. Shy, scared and shattered me was learning to stand up for her beliefs by being on her own feet to grow taller. I let myself make mistakes, which was something courageous. I was learning to let my feelings out, standing for my beliefs, and learning not to be afraid. Patience was the best part of the process. Patiently I was facing my fears and learning the positive statements to cleanse them. I was learning to accept the situations I did not expected. I learned to forgive myself.

I was restless and sleepless all the time. Meditating and spending many quiet times alone took so much of my time. I became isolated and kind of antisocial. During that time stage, I was playing Socrates on my own. Reading so many books and questioning people and relationships exquisitely was my new way of looking at life. This kind of isolated lifestyle became my new resolution. Mood swings and emotional turbulences kind of took me over but thought me a lot. My place started to grow up to be a sacred space. While my inceptions were growing to become more and more spiritual based.

I started to buy more icons, sculptures and totems and redecorated my apartment. As I changed my inner world, so did my outer world started to change. My house was reflecting me more. They were inspiring me better. My Christmas wishes were coming true. However, there was also something wrong within me. I was feeling tired, sleepless and heavy within me. Through those long hours of meditations and sleepless night was creating dark circles and pale skin. I was also having eczema attacks on my face. I was not sure what was causing all those discomfort and restlessness. I was only blaming my broken heart.

However I did not know that it was not only a broken heart but also a sick one.

Crystals and Symbols

I was daydreaming during the day. My morning walks became a routine. I started to come across some different kinds of stores. My favorite one was a natural stone store, which had many kinds of crystals. The owner was a geologist who was a very spiritual man. He showed me many different kinds of stones and thought me the various kinds of methods to use them for healing. So I started to work with crystals during my meditations. After working with crystals, I started to view some signs and symbols as I was in beta stage in my meditations. In order to learn the hidden meanings behind my visions, I started to note and draw them and start searching for their meanings.

Geologist in the natural stone store guided me on how to use my stones more efficiently in my meditations. He showed me the various healing and their cleansing methods. He always motivated me on finding my own ways to work on the crystals by working with them more everyday. So I tried. I laid the crystals on my body depending on the chakras they were representing during my meditations. I listened to crystal meditation music and imagined various different kinds of crystals while I was focusing on my chakras. I placed one hand on the main point of the chakra I was focusing on and was holding the crystal with my other hand in order to release the blockages in the areas. Additionally I was either reading or saying the positive affirmations of the chakras while I was holding the chakra stones.

As I got in the Beta stage of my meditation in which I was feeling deeply connected like in trans, I was seeing the symbols. I would be counting the symbols and meditate on the numbers. I was also visualizing the symbols and focusing on the crystals. They were leading me to my deep conscious levels. Therefore, the positive affirmations that I was saying before this stage was working more in a deeper level. As I was coming towards the end of my meditations I would be sending good intentions to my loved ones.

Crystals were helping me to calm down and ease my pain. I was feeling as if I was detoxifying my body. They were helping me to feel grounded. I was carrying them around me. The crystal shop had made a special crystal pendant with couple of different chakra stones held together. So I was carrying that pendant with me in my handbag. It was a chain with many colorful stones hanging down together. I was making my wish and carrying them around every day. As I was having those strange pressures within me, I was holding onto my pendant for grounding. At that time, I was not aware that I was feeling all those pressures because of my heart tumor but believed it to be depression. Surprisingly I was always choosing the pink rose crystals more than then other crystals for my meditations. My body knew what would be good for it self. Rose crystal is well known to be a healer for the heart chakra. Like it is said pink crystal was always helping to calm my tight squeeze in my heart.

I also chose to wear crystal pendants that would help to heal various parts of the body. Every time I wore them I hold the best intentions and said various positive affirmations. I generally chose to imagine myself totally happy and healthy. After using my crystals, I chose to cleanse them under running water. I sometimes used burning sage and held the crystals over them. This was helping to clear the energies in the house and also the stones. I put some crystals under my pillow before sleep such as amethyst or kyanite to ease me during sleep and help my dreams to be clearer. I took notes on my dreams in order to understand what was working better for me. I always held good intentions before applying these methods.

They all helped me and healed me. I am very thankful to the crystal shop owner who lead me for my choice in crystals and thought me their uses.

Healing Circle Meditation

Once a week I was creating a healing circle in front of my corner where I called to be my sacred space. My sacred space had my special Himalayan salt light; some icons were placed in it. It was peaceful and quiet with my favorite carpet laid in front of it for me to sit down for meditation. All my favorite icons, statues, lucky charms, the story that I wanted to create for myself were held in that space. Some prayers and beautiful greeting cards were hanged there. I would just breathe there and watch them with a smile on my face. It would always give me inspiration and peace. I would also create my healing circle in front of that space so that I can share the energy between the sacred space and the circle.

I would draw a huge circle, which is big enough for me to sit in the center. Than I would start placing my object on the circle. While I was doing it, I was repeating positive affirmations, good intentions, mantras or prayers in order to bring forth peace, love, healing and prosperity. Every time I was doing it I would choose a different prayer depending on my mood for the week. My objects were feathers I found on the street, snail shells, seashells, leaves, pinecones, candles, icons, praying beads with mantras, flowers, dried lavender, angelica, angel statues, and stones that I found on beach. Finally and most importantly I was placing chakra crystals in between the objects. After watching the circle for a while, I would find the music that would fit in to create a magical atmosphere. My dog would always get curious and come sniffing every each object that I would ask her to come and sit quietly next to me. We would than start praying for humanity, nature and unity.

My praying would continue as watching my thoughts for myself, my life, my family, my lover, my friends and my surrounding. Than I would choose to accept and love every each thought and never judge them as good or bad. If I needed to laugh I would. If I needed to cry, I would without questioning but just letting it all out. Little by little my breathing would slow down that I would forget everything. I would imagine my breathing as a healing energy cleansing my negativity and bringing in all higher energy frequencies. Then there would be silence and no clutter of thoughts but only peace in my heart. At that instance, I would create a huge imaginary clear crystal growing on top of my head and extending around my aura to heal the nature. I always knew that I was receiving a stronger energy back from nature. Energy would extend from my heart out to the Universe in a ray of Light. As much as I was open on receiving the love of the nature, I would be able to send as much love as I could. I would start sending love to myself, then the ones that I needed to forgive and lastly the ones that were there in my life.

When an instance comes to feel my surrounding, I would just open my eye and whatever object catches my eye I would send love to the first feeling that grows in me. Focusing on my energy between third dimension and fourth dimension in a beta stage. I would find myself imagining colorful clouds, dreaming of unicorns, Pegasus, Gods and Goddesses, strength of nature and than share the power of love with every one of each. This would follow by coming together with all my loved ones that I would feel as flying to stars. Shooting starts would pass us and I would choose a peaceful place and imagine gates that would take me to a beautiful garden.

When I step into my beautiful garden I would enjoy every each beauty of the nature. Watch every each flower and feel the nice warm breeze. Smell every each flower and exchange their healing energy. I would search for my favorite bank to sit on. My eyes would search through the beautiful garden to find all my loved ones that are waiting for me. Sometimes my guardian angels would greet us and watch over us. I would ask their allowance to join us. So then they would come and sit next to us. In their leadership and loving help I would have my own therapy or conversation between every each person. I would sit comfortably and quietly in our own privacy in order to exchange my wonderful loving thoughts with them. I would cleanse my negative thoughts and only turn everything into loving thoughts. Sometimes I would ask some acquaintances to appear in the garden so that I can ease the pain or create extra joy for the day so that I could find my balance. When I am done with my greetings with every each member, I would leave them in the garden knowing that I can always go back and share my energy.

During my meditations time I would put my phone on silence. Suprisingly all the people that I sent love during my meditations would call me during that time. They would text me letting me know that they missed me. When I called them back I would share my story with them and they would thank me because it would always be an answered prayer for all of us. I know that it was healing me as it was healing others as long as we were all connected.

After practicing different kinds of methods with crystals during my meditations, I cleaned my thyroid nodules. My doctors had given me medicines that I was obligated to have my whole life but I believed with prayer, positive affirmations, meditation and crystal therapy, everything could be healed. So I wore my blue quartz crystal everyday and meditated upon my throat. A year later my thyroids started to function healthy that doctors stopped my medication. Everybody was totally surprised accept me. I knew that through belief and positive thinking everything was possible.

'Impossible is nothing' as Muhammad Ali has said.

My chakra stones

I used black obsidian for my root chakra as long as it is the strongest stone but aragonite is also great one as long as it is a grounding stone. I sometimes used smoky quartz with them as well. For my second chakra I chose dark orange agate. I used citrine quartz and amber for the third chakra. Rose quartz and jade also worked good for my heart chakra. Fifth or throat chakra as I said previously; I used blue quartz, aquamarine, and also turquoise depending on my mood. Lapis lazuli is said to be the best and the only stone for third eye which is the sixth chakra. It would help to open psychic abilities and help you to have clairvoyance. I was holding the stone between my eyebrows during the meditation. Lastly amethyst and clear quartz is always good for the crown chakra. However, I always used my intuition when picking up my stones. I laid them on the ground in front of me as I said before and just picked them.

We should always remember that we are the healer for ourselves. All the stones and other kinds of applications are just tools that helps us to connect with our own self. So whatever you do as long as you hold good intentions and start with a positive mindset everything would be able to work for you. So I always held that knowledge within me and did whatever I felt like doing but also hold the knowledge that I heard or read around me. I chose to eat, drink and breathe with a good mindset. I was placing clear quartz next to my drinking water and every time I needed to fill my bottle I would say positive intentions and then drink my water. So the most important thing here was the choice that I made for myself, and then the intentions that I held for my choices.

When I traveled I only carried my clear quartz, which was good for every chakra and also black obsidian for protection. I sometimes carried small pieces of every each stone in my bag. Whenever I was in discomfort or under stress I just held my crystals. I held them, closed my eyes and took only three deep breathes, visualized my symbols than repeated some good intentions. Through years I started to collect stones, books about them. I became lovingly addicted to my stones by adoring them.

I want to share my story of how I started to be curious about crystals. I was always wearing natural stones such as jade since my early ages but did not heard about crystals. I remember myself wearing an amber ring when I was in high school. I believed in its luck during my exams. Surprisingly I found out later that amber was a great stone for memory and cleansing. Therefore it is always good to use intuition when picking up your stone. As I said I always liked the stones and was always interested in them but knew them only as gemstones. I never heard the word crystal until I met my last boyfriend. One day in order to explain his feelings for me. He said that I was like a precious crystal store and he was like an elephant that was not able to fit in it. I was so touched with this statement. He was telling me how innocent and clear I was in my relations. I started to wonder where I could find crystals and study their appearance. I wished to find one and look at it closely in order to see how he sees me in them. Next day I met with the geologist and found his store filled with crystals. I was like an elephant every time I walked into that small store. Than crystals went into my life and I started to collect them since that day.

Through time I learned that crystals, symbols, oracle cards, or any other kind of healing method was just a tool between the higher self and me. They were a bridge or a communication tool for me to find my capability. As long as I believed in me and hold the highest vision of myself than everything was possible. There was a higher guidance that was showing me the possibilities and I had the free will to choose. Whatever I choose it would be the best for me. The worst and the best was equal as long as I had my growth lessons. Trusting the self and holding the faith would create the miracles. Meanwhile choosing to use the tools that the nature has laid upon us would help us to hear our higher self, hidden inside.

Research

I bought so many books about Atlantis, Island Mu, Egypt, India and specific books on signs and symbols. More and more I was working on these symbols; I started to come across much more of them. They were answering the questions I held on my mind. Randomly reading them has helped me to find meaning in my researches. I had always been a perfectionist when it came to reading books. I would start from the introduction page and read through the last page. However with the latest books I chose I was just randomly opening pages and finding the information I was looking for. I was clearer with my research and information I received. Crystals kind of opened my receptivity. I started to have clairvoyance about information that I never heard of. My instincts grew stronger. Through time it grew stronger and stronger.

I was looking for information on the symbols that I would have a meaning for my dreams and meditations. Infinity symbol was coming across me all the time. Therefore I decided to carry it with me. I had it tattooed on my wrist. I believed tattoo and the process always had a spiritual meaning. In ancient times all the great Indian tribes and also old traditional Turkish tribes whose ancestors are believed to be the Indians always tattooed themselves with symbols. So placing triangle and infinity symbols brought more meaning into my life. It helped me to believe in my symbolic guidance more, and go further deeper into my researches. I read about shamanism, tribal ceremonies, different kinds of healing methods, Chinese methods, Greek Mythology, Gods and Goddesses, various religions and practices. My vision grew wider so did my perspective on self. I started to become more curious about my past.

I did lots of Internet research as well. I searched on animals and their symbolic meanings in dreams and also in real life. I was coming across the same animal on the street such as crows, snails, frogs, pigeons, or any other animal as finding pictures of them. I used whats-your-sign.com when I was curious about the meanings of animals and symbols. Avia Venefica was a great source of information for me. Her website is amazing. As she said 'Life is symbolic. Start interpreting.' I did through her website and my books.

Animal totems

One day I saw a store with a unicorn sculpture for display, which is a very difficult mystical animal symbol you would find in Turkey. Therefore, it grabbed my attention. I have been longing to have a unicorn in my house so I went into the store to look for it. As soon as I entered in, I realized it was a mystic store with a incent smell. They were selling oracle cards, stones, tarot cards, and self-improvements books, healing bowls, icons, crystals and more. They were giving tarot readings and life coaching. I was so interested with everything they had and had too much knowledge and curiosity on their subjects that the owner whom never came out of his room did finally came out to meet me. After we met, I became more interested with the store that I decided to go there almost once a week. I believed at the time my guiding spiritual animal was a unicorn so it guided me to the store, which held all the information I needed.

The storeowner was going abroad and was bringing many different kinds of crystals. I learned many types of crystals. I also bought my book about crystals called Crystal Bible in that store which gave me the chance to learn various uses of the stones. The storeowner and I started to have long spiritual conversations. That store became my stepping-stone and motivation. The storeowner became a very good friend of mine. His name is Özügür, which means having a strong core.

My first introduction to oracle cards and Viking runes came to me because of him. He was selling Doreen Virtue's Goddess oracle cards as well. Through those cards I learned more Goddesses and different kinds of beliefs all across the globe. I did more research and applied them into my meditations and even into my paintings. On the other hand, getting introduced to Viking runes has changed my life. The symbols on the runes were very spiritual and meaningful to me. They were also very similar to old ancient Turk alphabet. I was so amazed when realizing that the traditions, symbols and believes were so similar and connected to each other. After practicing the runes for a long time, I became very familiar with them. Also keeping a diary has opened my consciousness and awareness. I realized after a certain of time that runes were very familiar to Tarot reading. Vikings used these runes before going to battles, long distance travels and also for their spiritual practices as guidance.

After making the connection between the Viking runes and Turk Alphabet, I decided to apply them to my work. I used the runes as symbols in my paintings. Later I applied them to my performances. All the viewers took notes about the symbols and their meanings. It was a tribute for me to the Goddesses and Vikings. I was introduced to their world and had so many awakening moments that distributing the information to my viewers became a life purpose to me. Introducing the spiritual information to the interested viewer was an awarding experience for me.

Tarot and 6 Degrees

Özügür was also giving tarot readings that I dared to take his reading couple of times. All I wanted was to familiarize myself with cards and the reading. My dream was to have my own cards and learn to read them for myself in the future.

He explained me the meaning of Tarot reading and its uses. He laid the cards in front of me in different kinds of methods. I felt that he was using the cards through his instincts. He was also learning them every each day. His self was teaching him. We were all beginners. His experiences just thought him some more through time. I was there not to learn the cards but to learn the secrets of his wisdom. He was very open to my interpretations. He wanted to see the laid cards through the eye of an artist. It was as if we were both feeding each other with information and learning together.

There was a reason for us to come across. I knew from the beginning that our meeting in his store was not just a coincidence. He was sent to me with a Divine purpose. He was helping me to open my spiritual side and always motivating me. He was always encouraging me to believe in myself. Maybe we were going through the same process of life at that time that we came across. Both of us needed to learn the same during that time. His readings were sometimes like his own readings he would say. His guidance was always towards finding self and connecting with my higher self. So he thought me to pay attention to my self and trust my instincts. Every time he saw me he would say that I was more curious and more connected. He helped me to see where I was standing at the time. He helped me to be more aware of myself and live life more consciously.

He only gave me two readings but it was a stepping-stone for me at its time. The most important lesson he had given me was to acknowledge me about human connections. He said the Universe connected to us through the connection of five people, including the first person as I, it would become six people. This was called Six Degrees of Connection. Anyone that you would like to meet around the globe, you only needed to find five people of connection. In order to find those five people, you only needed to concentrate on your goal and let the spirit do the rest. The work of magic is just to let go and be aware when you meet people. Six Degrees of Connection became the stepping-stones for me. I listened to him carefully and wanted to apply it in every area of my life. Even learning a new idea and letting the Universe work its magic was a great success. All I need to do was to believe in this unity and connection. Afterwards strong wish and patience that came from trust would lead me to my desired person. He asked me to try this for fun. He said we were all connected and united that there was not any single person on Earth that we would not meet. So I just decided to try it for fun.

That day I asked the Universe to help me find my 6 Degrees of Connection in order to meet Madonna. Madonna was an iconic person who lived in United States, very popular and very hard to reach 'an impossible' to me. Well I was mistaken. She is a superstar so I smiled at my self when I desired to meet her. That summer Madonna came to Istanbul to give a concert after 20 years. The last time I went to her concert was when I was in primary school. I wanted to go to the concert but did not have the tickets. It was impossible to get tickets for her concert. I did not even try to get and I was not a big fan of her anyways.

I went to my parents' house for the weekend. We were all sitting together and talking about our daily activities. Suddenly my mother turned to me and directly asked me if I would like to go with her to Madonna concert. My mother made me a surprise and got me tickets without telling me. This was my first surprise when I found out that she got the tickets. She said she reserved the tickets from months ago that she had the hottest tickets.

A week before the concert, I found out that I had a very important event that I had to attend that I had a to sell the Madonna tickets. It was fine for me. I was never too excited for anything. The concert would be too crowded for me anyways. Madonna tickets were sold out and would be very easy for me to sell. So there was nothing to worry. I was asking around to sell my tickets. One night I was invited to one of my best friends house for coffee. We were talking and the conversation came to my adventure about selling the concert tickets. They asked me if I would go to concert. I said I was not a fan of her, had the tickets as a gift but I had to attend a meeting that I had to sell them. They looked at each other and told me that they had VIP tickets. I asked them how and as long as we were best friends they knew me that they wanted to share their story.

My friend looked at her husband, smiled and gave him a nod to proceed with the story. They said that they were friends with Madonna so that they had VIP tickets as a gift personally from her. They even received a call from her asking them to give her a quick city tour. It was their weird secret that they asked me to keep. I was shocked not because they knew Madonna but that I really had the connection to Madonna as I requested. My best friend's husband knew Madonna and was talking about giving Madonna a private tour. He was one of my 6 degrees of connection. So the six people connection was for real. My friends realized that I was not so surprised and was not so held back about them knowing her. So they were very pleased and happy. I did not question their history with the star. I respected their privacy and secret. Only thing that mattered to me was to understand how 6 Degrees of Connection work so that I could apply it in any degree of my life.

The next week I saw my best friend and his husband giving Madonna a private tour on the newspapers. It was quiet funny to see them next to the superstar. She did not look like a superstar to me any longer. I understood that nobody was that important. We were all humans. Ego was the only issue making people look important. It was a huge moment that put a lightning on top of my head. I was just smiling at the newspaper with a dazzle in my eyes. I had a stupid smile on my face the whole day.

The next week I found out that another friend of mine was selling bags to Madonna. So I got used to the idea and stopped testing the six connections but only focus on the person I really desired to meet. However there was none. This experience only helped me to understand that if only you held good intentions and pay attention to your desired outcome than there was no reason for you not to have it. Only thing you needed was to ask for it and than trust it. Divine timing would bring it to you.

Your desire could be meeting Madonna or just finding the right doctor for your health. So I decided to use this power of 6 Degrees of Connections for good reasons. Life showed me in the coming future how I had my 6 Degrees of Connection to find cure for my heart.

CHAPTER IV

Signs from above

In the late hours of the night, I started to search on the Internet mainly looking for the signs, symbols and their use in the ancient times. During this time my eye was constantly seeing the time in repetitious numerological forms. This kind of coincidences was usually beginning at 11:11 than continuing as 12:12 and on and on. It was kind of scary for me at the beginning as long as it was happening every each night while I was searching on unusual subject matters. I tried to share these instances with my friends but their responses were generally strange and unusual. It was hard for them to believe. Most of them thought I was making up these stories or having artistic creativity moments. Some people started to joke that I was crazy. They were telling me to be reasonable and less daydreaming. So I basically did not have enough friends to share but I know universe would send me when I needed. So it did.

The Universe was helping me not through friends but the people I started to meet in the shop I went into. My

introduction to Oracle cards and Viking Runes changed
my life and helped to be clearer on the questions I had. I
started to use them to receive answers. I was becoming so
amazed at the beginning but Özügür thought me to stop
getting surprised and let myself see all the experiences as
an answered prayer to my strong instincts. He cautioned
me not to share my experiences with every other but only
with my self. However, I knew that I would share them
one day. My cards helped me to understand nature spirit
and read the symbols in nature. I learned through my
readings that nature was sending me signs by leaving
feathers on the street in front of me. Butterflies were
there to tell me to be strong. Cats were there to remind
me my independence and enjoy life. Seashells were there
to protect my home. Crystals were for healing. Gathering
leaves from the nature and using their scents were good
for my soul. Therefore, I paid attention to them.

As I learned to look for feathers as a symbol for
angelic help, I realized I was not alone. I started to see
them around my house. I was questioning their reality
but still longing to believe in them. One day I woke up
and got ready to take a walk. When I stepped outside
my apartment I was shocked. The whole street was filled
with white feathers. A man with a brush was trying to
clean them up but they were still all around. I told it to
my mother and she asked me not to be ridiculous. She
said it was the season for the bird to loose feathers. I was
so devastated that I decided not to ask anyone but only
use my own senses. Maybe Özügür was right to caution
me that it was not a good time to share these kind of

magical information with anybody because they were discouraging me.

I was changing for good and my circle of friends and my family members were not there for me yet. The time would come for them to understand me one day too. I told myself that I was not alone. I was going through perception that was teaching me to understand. Next day, my mother called me. She sounded so excited and surprised on the phone. She told me that she visited the street that I lived and realized that there were so many white feathers laying in front of my apartment but not on the other streets that she walked. She said she was so surprised that she could not give a meaning. I was so heartbroken with her reaction that I chose to stay silent. The following days feathers were gone. I realized that they were there to tell me that angels were real and they were trying to tell me that I was not alone. I had their support all around me. So I decided to ask God and angels to send me feathers whenever I needed for guidance.

Afterwards I started to pick feathers on the streets to put into my healing circle. During my meditations I put them in my circle with stones, shells, oak tree pieces and crystals in order to send healing love and light to my home and surrounding. I started to do it more as a way to thank nature.

Entering 4ᵗʰ Dimension

Numbers strange game on me continued. My search on the Internet provided resources related to 11:11 and 12:12 explaining them as wake-up calls. All the related articles written on these numerical coincidences were meant to be signals from the soul. I felt strange but also confident on what I was doing. I felt inside that I was receiving some messages. Only thing I needed was to pay attention to the signs. I was so close to the source, which made me feel strange.

I was looking for answers everywhere but it was right under my hand after I really concentrated and asked for it. I realized that Internet was the real source. All the resources that I needed to know about the spirit was coming in front of me corresponding to the energy field I was working on. I felt like I was connected to high frequencies.

The articles were mainly talking about the magnetic waves that our thought process creates on the net, which was able to connect with the quantum leaps so that it would help us to get connected with our psychic abilities. It was the sign of the spirit that were orchestrated by Elohim. It was an energy that was working with many other people on the computer field through the information system. When you get the messages as a call, you were choosing yourself by completing the subjects in need in order to help the brothers and sisters of the earth in the circle of oneness. It was a call to help the ones to be awakened to realize the spirit and yet be a better soul by helping through this process. It was said that it was a way to show the quantum energy field to the people.

Mainly 11:11 was a sign, a waking call for the people to come together as Light workers and use this high frequency in order to understand the meaning of source.

All the articles were talking about the same subject and the need for the Light workers to bring peace and harmony to this earth by working on the energy field by receiving the high frequencies of energy and grounding it to earth to bring peace. The experiences of people were shared on the Internet on how these numerological signs were connecting people together. It was talking about how people saw these numeric assistances after their meditations. They explained their stories about how they applied them into their lives. I was very excited to find people with similar stories. It encouraged me to move on.

After I continued on reading I became more aware of what I was reading. My fears and questions started to surface as if I needed to be cleansed. As I kept searching on more and more subjects through my readings, I started to come across subjects that were causing my fear to rise. At the end, I decided to get over my fears and concentrate on what I should face. So instead of declaring myself as an insane person and being afraid of ending up crazy, I decided to face everything. I decided to accept my self and being. I told myself that there was nothing to be afraid but only accept what was there for me. So I calmed down, prayed and I continued.

After I accepted this and decided to continue, many strange pop-up ads started to come on my computer screen, which was impossible to happen as long as my computer was Mac and locked to advertisements. Than I used my inner senses to open pages and follow some pages and took some notes related to my instincts. At the end when I put the notes together, it was giving me signs not to be afraid of anything as long as I was always protected. All I wanted was to search more and feel the peace of the presence. I made notes of some dates where I would learn some new insights on spiritual matters of my heart and relationships. Than there were some images on swords, maps and battles which I noted. I realized they were all kinds of information related to my ancestors.

The next day, I called my grandmother and asked her about my great grandparents and ancestors' life story. I was very surprised to find out that the dates, the information I came across and notes that I took were same with the information my grandmother was giving me. I learned that her husband was a soldier that attended navy and travelled to the places that I marked on the map. All these information made me more curious and less afraid. I stopped worrying if I was going mad instead I realized I had strong instincts that could help me on my journey with the self. All I needed was to share them when the right time comes.

Entering 5th Dimension

I started to search the meaning of the numbers. I was not sure what was going on at the time. So I typed in 12:12 on the search engine and a long list of information came out. I started to go through them and realized there were many people experiencing what I have been going through. The meaning of 12:12 was a call on Elohim and the need for great awakening. It was a door to the fifth dimension. Some said that on the year 2012 the doors for the fifth dimensions energy would be open on 12.12.12. I found a very long document explaining the process by giving the history, ancestors, related seekers and also how to become the chosen one.

The document was basically asking the ones who come across numbers to make a commitment to continue the work on seeking self, spirit and life mission by reading on the steps in the documents towards the end. It was an agreement that was carried from Melchizedek's time. I was very unfamiliar with the terms so that I found a big leather notebook, which was looking like old ancient notebooks and started to scratch the terms in them. At the end of the night, the notebook was half filled with signs, notes, and drawings. I was looking at it with my half mouth open, and at the same time questioning myself if I was going crazy.

As I was reading towards the end of the paragraphs, topics began to turn out strange as if it knew what I would be doing next. At one point I read that 'Dear friend do not question your sanity and do not be afraid, you have walked upon this path with great patience so be ready for more surprises. If you were willing to continue on after meeting your next biggest surprise, you would be blessed to choose to continue on this path.' I was shocked and decided to give a break and have a cup of tea to relax. I returned back to keep on reading and it said now you have made your hot tea. I gave a big scream. I thought I was being watched so I put the lights off. However, there was something pulling me towards the computer so I decided not to stop but keep on reading because I was questioning if I understood it right. It continued as warning me not to be afraid but stay patient as the lights will go off, the blue lights will come up.

At that instant, the electricity went off and I had seen some blue lights outside my building. I did not know what was going on but I found it not usual. I gave up on questioning whether I understood it right or wrong because I read it several times. I decided to come out of my building and all the lights inside the building were blue as well. The sirens went on as long as the electricity was off and the alarms were turned on automatically. I decided to get out of my apartment three in the morning and walk a little bit to calm down.

I looked up and saw the group of my lucky stars right above my head. I took a big breath and said to myself that there is nothing to be afraid here. I am only overcoming my fears and this is just a small fair play of life to me. Life is only reflecting my inner self to me. So take a big breath, believe in yourself and walk into your apartment. So I did. I accepted all as my illusion and decided not to think on it further but just live the moment at its own pace. At that instant I understood the game of illusion in three-dimensional life of mine. I still did not know whether I understood the reading as I wanted to understand or it was a call for me to wake-up from above but I felt more faithful and connected afterwards. Maybe that night was all I needed to come across my fears.

At the end of the night, I looked at the reading and it said congratulations you are shedding your old parts and becoming one of us. I continued on reading and taking notes. When the morning came and the sun was coming up, I was at the end of my reading. Whether I understood its true meaning or manipulated it, I experienced what I had to experience in order to grow to become a better self. After that day I never found that reading again. There were bunch of people that I sent the reading to but not many of them received it. The ones that received it did not understand the language of it.

The next day I found a huge collage of work posted on my wall with drawings. I realized I was not only drawing my notebook but at the same time cutting and pasting papers on my wall. Maybe it was my artistic creativity that arouse during that night. I was so hyper that I did so many things that I could not follow. I knew what I was doing but I did not know how it looks. The next days when my friends came to visit my house, they did not notice the posts on the walls. It probably did not grab their attention. The people whom has noticed them and understood were the ones who shared similar experiences with me and were interested in the same matters of the heart. They never questioned but only shared their own similar stories.

CHAPTER V

Clairvoyance

As these strange connections were happening in my life. I decided not to wear a watch to see the time but instead feel my own reality of time. I realized time was only an illusion we created depending on the ancients creation of time. I put down all the clocks in my house. I promised myself not to live by chasing time but only feeling my body's need towards time. I thought it was what time sequences were trying to tell me. It was working out very well for me. I was neither later nor missing any appointment. Happiness was all over me.

The next day a friend of mine called me. Without knowing what was happening new in my life, she started to talk about number 11 and 12 as in dimensional sequences of life and taking them as good or bad spirits entering into our lives. I decided not to question her information but only take every thing in a positive matter. Energy levels were such a sensitive subject matter that it was very easily to be put down by creating negative thinking. Universe was always sending us our mirror through people in order for us to face our hopes and fears. Challenges were facing us all through time but we only needed to see them as a game of illusion instead of an examination. So I decided that either good or bad whatever was happening in my life was only happening for my highest benefit. Everything that was happening in my life was only growth lesson for me. At first it would be very hard for me to take this attitude in to my life style but through time I would learn to digest and benefit from this idea. I needed to drop my control issues and let the spirit interfere with my life.

At that point any given information on evil or good would put me up or down. I promised myself not to let any energy vampire to sabotage my senses. Patience was the key in my learning process. I just should not be afraid of them, get surprised by them or question them much but accept them as they were so that they would continue steering into my life.

The numbers continued on following me. I was coming across 11, 12 or 13 at the door numbers, license plates, street numbers and more. When I decided to let it go, challenge was harder. Universe was sending me more information to face my self. I tried not to ignore license plates but than phone numbers would appear in front of me. Sometimes the digital clocks would stop by it self and change automatically on a repetitive number that did not make any sense of the time at that moment. I only continued my usual life and tried to stay calm.

One day I met a very close friend of mine whom I knew since college. We were kind of distant in our friendship at the beginning but through years my interest in spirituality and hers kind of connected us. She was the only one that I was able to share my thoughts and experiences. We kind of shared similar interests that we were able to come together and discuss these matters. On that day she told me that she was also seeing the same number on the streets she walked. She told me that the number 69 kept appearing in her life. It would be on license plates, doors and phone numbers she came across. We entered into a small coffee shop and our conversation was generally on her experiences. When we came out of the shop, she notices that the building's number was 69. We were both thrilled and started to laugh so hard. We said goodbye and she stopped a cab to head back home. Surprisingly, its license plate number was again 69. Universe has sent me the help by sending my best friend with the same question in her mind so that we both would search on the meaning.

At night she gave me a call telling me that she did an Internet research and came across Doreen Virtue, who wrote about number sequences on a blog and explained their meaning. She had given a list of repeating numbers and explained the term as numerology. The meaning hidden behind the number she sees was exactly about the concerns she was having in her life at that time. I asked my friend to send the blog address to me. So she did. As soon as I read it, I was relieved. I realized I was not making things up but people were really experiencing the same awkward situations and calling them blessings as I did. Doreen Virtue was a PHD and she was contacting with angels through numbers.

Afterwards numbers became a subject for me to receive messages and I decided to work on them more often to heal my life. They helped me to be more connected to my inner self and find the solutions within my self other than outside sources. I learned to trust my self and my life's challenges. I stopped resisting them but facing them as blessings and great life lessons.

<u>My collages with numerology</u>

I started to note my findings and numbers in my dearest notebook. I started to cut and paste things that were important to me. Every time I read or learned a matter on the Internet toward spirit, I was writing in my notebook. When I had questions about them, I was randomly shuffling through the pages of books and coming across answers. Later, they started to reflect on my paintings as well.

During long sleepless nights, I started to make big collage works on paper. I did not have enough material to cut and paste that I was running out of them. All I needed was some more magazines. I just wished hard to find them in order to reflect my callings. The next morning, I opened my door to get the morning paper and found a big bag filled with the best foreign magazines inside. I realized that my up-stair neighbor without knowing what I was looking for decided to give his old magazines to me. He thought an artist would always need extra materials. I was so cheerful and happy. I realized that through this search in the magazines I would start to receive messages about my life mission.

Through a four months process, I created more than twelve collages. They were 150x100 meters in length with mix media cut and pasted from magazines, newspapers and found objects that I found meaningful to share. During the working process, I was going through a transit. I would not be able to explain it with words but only paint in various stories that I would call fairy tales that I wanted in my life. Some has happened after I finished them and some did not but they were all so meaningful to me. They were like storyboards that I wanted to create in life. Each of them brought various different signs that I explained as various messages of the spirit. They were given to me to follow in order to hear my heart.

Some nights I would watch the stars and their positions, read some books related on them, draw their various positions on my paintings. Some days I would work on healing crystals and Kryon's crystal symbols and apply them on the collages in order to bring peace and harmony into my life, relationships and all the other people that I was related to. They were each very strong pieces with strong messages that I would not even understand after I finish. I was starting by concentrating on a single number that I came across a lot during that day. By painting the number on the paper I would ask for a message and a meaning for me to follow to share with others.

After focusing on the number, I would search through my material. As I turned the pages of the magazines the pictures or headlines would follow like a storyline. I would just cut and paste them in an order I see and place them on the craft paper. I was writing notes on them to remember what was going on. All the messages were like answered prayers that were helping me to choose the next material. All the colors and numbers had hidden messages reflecting my transfer between subconscious to conscious level. I started to keep all the finished work hidden in a room that no other person would see and call me crazy. I was just working on them to see my callings and felt that later in time I would learn the meaning behind the process. Believed that when the time comes, it would tell me what to do.

Positive Manifestations

I was meditating every night and sending my manifestations, my dreams, and also my wishes to Universe. I was not putting my wishes into phrases but leaving it open to manifest it self so that whatever good will come to me in perfect timing. I had a trust in Divine timing and also my self. I always tried not to frame them but live it open so that Divine Force would enter in to bring the better one for me. Having specific expectations in life did never worked for me. The reason was that I was not the person to know what would be the best for me. I was only believing in Universe and saying that whatever was good would always come to me in its highest form. Therefore I was only concentrating on using positive affirmations in a general form so that I was implying as it already becoming in my life.

I was telling myself that all is good even if I believed that something was not good. I always told myself that I am in love with life and my self even if my love relationship was not going well. I believed that life would push the reality directly in front of me and by the time I realize it I would choose to change my life in the best choice. So I was repeating my self that all the best solutions are within me. If I were afraid that I was not capable I would repeat that I am whole and adequate to be capable of anything. Repeating the words of trust, faith and love always creates the strongest energy field for my unity. Telling self that I am full with love and faith.

At the time, I needed to sign up with a gallery that would be friendly, peaceful and also prosperous for my own needs. Most importantly, I was looking for a kind atmosphere that would bring harmony to my work. One night after long hours of meditation in my healing circle, I had an urge to follow my instincts. When I was done, I walked to my living room and sat beside my light globe as I felt like. I closed my eyes, turned the globe and placed my index finger on top of a place that I had never heard of. I opened my eyes and it was an island in the north poles. I looked what was written on the place and it said Elizabeth bay, which was very much like angel shaped with a flute in a hand. I did not know why I chose to do that action but felt it like a sign so I decided to write my finding down. I thought I might receive some good news as long as an angel image was holding the flute. I thought to myself the flute was a symbol for a message. All I needed was to be patient and have trust in my instincts. Something good was going to come along its way, I felt it. One day a gallery owner wanted to come for a visit to my studio with her assistant. I accepted the offer with pleasure and asked for their name. When I heard the answer, I had a huge smile on my face. Her name was Elizabeth.

She was a very friendly and positive minded person who brought sunshine to my studio. At the first instance I knew that I would work with her. She had a brand new gallery with a great reputation, which was more than good for me. All I wanted was somewhere that I would feel free and longing. Their gallery was full of energy. The building that the gallery was located was called Crystal. What more I could ask. The signs were written all over them. I believed there was magic in Elizabeth and her place also would bring me the luck I was looking for. She had a very pleasant smile and warm attitude towards me.

Elizabeth spent many long hours in my studio with her wonderful conversations not only in arts but also in her life that would inspire me. All her views about life were very similar to mine. She was laughing all the time and kept smiling that made me feel very comfortable and peaceful at the same time. She had a very positive attitude. After she examined my work she told her interest in them. Later she wanted to follow me to the back room, where I stored my paintings, in order to see my older works. We started to go through the canvases but in an instant something grabbed her attention. I had my collage work hidden under my couch but one of their corners were peaking out as if the paper works wanted to come out. She said she was curious with them that she wanted to see them.

As soon as I took them out she became breathless. She found them full of energy and asked me to put them in a show. She wanted the collage works to be in the first floor of the gallery and the canvases on downstairs of the gallery. I was so surprised and accepted her offer as long as she was a very experienced lady. I believed that she would know the best for my work and me. She took her time examining the details of each work and asked me many questions. She looked over the symbols, numbers and writings that I put on every each paper work. She said she found herself in them and believed everyone would also feel the same. Elizabeth wanted me not to be shy about those works but share it with everyone. So she asked me to continue on my work and let her know when I was done. I loved her trust in me. So that I gave her my promise that I would never let her down. It took me couple of months more to complete the series, which were taking a night to finish.

I also wanted to make a catalogue with my poems for every each collage, but I was not able to start writing them. One night, a week before the exhibition, I took a deep breath. I closed my eyes and dreamed every each day I painted them. I felt what I have learned from every each of them. I evaluated myself in those moments. Realized how much information I had processed into the work. All the books and researches ran in front of my eye. Like a movie scene my couple of months flew in front of me.

Sezin Aksoy

I laid every collage in front of me. Sat in front of them and just started to write a poem without thinking but only concentrating on their numbers and story. Thirteen poems came out for each painting in one night. It was as if something else was letting me write all the lines in the poems instead of me. I was only letting it pour out of me. It was like a cleansing for me. When I was done, I felt a huge relief.

The exhibition went so well. The show was sold out. People had goose bumps when they saw the work. I had a very good feedback. The exhibition was on the news. Everybody was talking about it. I met so many beautiful people. They came to me and told me that they had similar experiences. Some said the paintings reminded them their deceased loved ones. Some said the work reminded them of the messages they received from the angels. So many likeminded people gathered in the gallery without knowing the new work or me. I was so excited and grateful. I was so thankful to all the information that came in front of me through the process of creation. I felt so responsible for all the connection I made. It was a blissful day.

My friends told me that I was lost for months but came out like a shine. I was so happy that my dreams came true. However, there was some trouble in me that needed to be completed. I felt like some of the paintings were trying to tell me something that I have not understood at that time. It was not only success I was looking for but also having a faithful companion whom would always be there for me. I was very grateful to the love I received from life but I needed someone to complete me. I needed a partner to share my happiness. I needed that kind of peace in my heart but it was not there.

Calling on Nature Spirits

I continued on doing my meditations and prayers. I would create my healing circle and call on the nature spirits, Ascended Masters. I was working with them unconsciously in order to heal my energy field to bring me a better level of awareness. I would let nothing to put me down. I was so grateful for the prosperity I had in my life. All the angels were on my side. I never felt alone. So I knew all was well and would be better.

During my meditations I would clear my chakras and focus on my positive affirmations. My sacred space I created always reflected my desires I was manifesting on. So that, I placed pictures of nature and flowers, had flower essences, aroma therapeutic oils, incense sticks related to the pictures around the house. Candles were always lit at night. Sometimes I would keep one candle lit all night to remind me to keep my faith in the morning. After relaxing with deep breathing methods, I would meditate on mantras I read. I would repeat them silently and when I was ready I would send the love and light to myself, than my loved ones, friends, and people I met and did not meet. I would ask for my worries to be lifted so that I would be free of stress. As I was coming towards the end, I would concentrate on one matter that was very dear to my heart, something that I needed guidance. I would ask my question very deep within and let it flew in the air.

When I was ready I had clairvoyance, first as a light circling in front of my eyes changing into symbols lastly into numbers. At the beginning I was checking on the meaning of the numbers on numerology. Through time I learned their meaning and started to interpret them on my own. Depending on the people I concentrated on I wrote the numbers down as dates that their concerns would be solved. Most of them were accurate. This made me happier than I imagined. So I dedicated myself more to my meditations. They improved my life.

I was sending love and light to the authors that helped me to understand the meanings. All the motivations I received from their writings inspired me. I felt courage towards my goals and my abilities. I learned to trust myself and become more independent on my choices. This made me feel stronger emotionally and spiritually which I needed the most in my life.

Every time I meditated I would start by calling on the Nature Spirit to be with me. I would concentrate on my guiding animal to show me the way and the plants, incents and trees to be with me. I will be sending my love and gratitude towards them and always invite them to my energy field. I believed in their protection, guidance and courage to let me move on. In return I always respected nature. I decided to change the cleaning products I used in my house. I started to pick the environment friendly products. I started to recycle and also use canvas bags instead of plastic bags. Whenever I saw litters around my parents' house near the trees; I started to pick them. One day I saw an old couple having their morning walk near the forest and saw me picking litters. They looked at me with a big surprising faced that I felt ashamed a little bit but never minded them. They stopped and told me that they were very proud of seeing a youngster like me. I felt happy that they were proud of me and thought that I was a teenager.

CHAPTER VI

Wakeup call

The whole summer was ahead of me. I started my new paintings. I became more aware of my needs and desires. I started to pay more interest in painting animals by emphasizing their symbolic meanings. Crows began to play an important role in my life. I started to see them around my house and neighborhood. Hear their wonderfully strong sound. They were kind of communicating with me. Black feathers on their skin were shining and reflecting many tones of black and blue. I admired their beautiful color and elegant shape. As they flew around and landed on a tree, they were like flying through time and coming from ancient years. They were so wise and old spirited. Their eyes had meaning carrying ancient stories that I was longing to see and listen.

I watched their moves, attitudes and communication. Their figure was sharp like drawn with black ink. As I spent time looking at them, I became drawn into their motion. Their skinny legs and long nails were grabbing into my balcony bar and making tiny sounds when they moved up and down. Their beak was like pair of sharp scissors. Every time they opened them to shout, their body was growing intense and they seemed like shouting from the gut. Spending long hours searching for them in my garden made me so excited. One day, I decided to leave it to the spirits to send the crows to me when I needed. So I started to look into the sky and send my blessings to the wind and the crows. I asked them to communicate within me by their strong sound and give me message through their tone. I know that they are a sign for long life and good fortune so that I always look around to find them.

In the mornings, I began waking up with their long shouts. In very early hours of the mornings they started to come to my window. Maybe they needed their space and trust and were evaluating mine. In order to build a strong relationship with them, I had to let it go. Not only people but also animals needed their space. So I paid them my tribute. They were screaming with joy asking me to wake up and celebrate the day. I did not care what time it was. I only looked at time to see if the numbers were also trying to communicate with me. Mentioning me to use my inner senses. I called Athena to help me get tuned into my natural spirits with her wisdom. So I left my warm bed, walked in front of the window and watched them for hours.

Afterwards I walked to my desk and opened my diary and started to draw the beautiful shapes of them. I draw them with black pencil as if they were shadows of the trees. They were gathered on top of linden trees in my apartment's garden. In pairs they were flying from one branch to another. Crows looked seriously happy. They thought me to take this life serious. I should know their story. I should hear their cries. We were all free. We had freedom of choice. We only needed to choose happiness and joy in life instead of fear. If only we appreciate life, we would be independent. Every morning was bliss and every night was a blessing. When the night ends morning would always come but only if you believe in it.

One day I saw a left red balloon stuck on one of the branches of tall trees. Crows were staring into each other. They were flapping their wings and watching the wind. They looked like melodies on the music scales communicating between each other. I thought to myself that I might have been a crow in one of my previous lives. So the next day, I decided to paint a crow on my canvas. It was all in red and one big crow shouting out melodies. I prayed for it to bring love and harmony to my life.

Peaceful mornings

I would take my tea outside and have my breakfast in my small narrow balcony. Smelling the linden trees in the morning breeze woke my senses. Looking way up in the sky and asking my nature spirits to talk to me was my morning ritual. Asking them to send me a crow with a message. I waited in long minutes and only listened to the breeze. I heard the leaves shaking. Small linden flowers were puffing in the air. Sun was lighting them with many different colors. I was seeing many different colors in them as if they were crystals. They were sparkling in the summer breeze.

I had goose bumps all over me when I heard the birds singing. They were orchestrating a ceremony for the nature. Love and light was in the air. Balance and harmony was there for me to sniff. Inhaling all the peace, exhaling all my troubles, learning from tunes of nature and sending my gratitude. Than like a magic one big crow would flew and landed onto the big branch right in front of me. Moving to its sides in small left and right steps. In order to decide what to do looked around very carefully. I thought it would just fly away like it did in the previous days. Suddenly my messenger crow has jumped to my balcony bar while I was sitting there. Beautiful black crow looked into my eyes and gave a sharp long quaking sound. I knew at that time that my wish would come true. I only wanted it to be in a blissful manner.

Every morning hearing crows or seeing them in my balcony started to bring me good news. I read somewhere that paying attention to crows tune and recording them in a diary would help the listener to interpret the symbolic meanings hidden behind every sound. As it said in the article, I started to watch them very closely and record their sounds. Sometimes they were crying out only once, sometimes twice and when they did more they would be angry at something.

Cats climbing up to the trees would stare at the crows and made them make the quaking sound several times. I started to decode their sound and hear their calling to other crows. Paying more and more attention to them changed my life. They brought so much joy to my life. My senses grew stronger with them. They were like wake up calls to me.

Past lives

Hearing caws and listening to them had magic in them. I was feeling peaceful. My best friend whom I had really long conversations about animals, symbols and meditation was very dear to me. She would come any time I called her and we would meditate for hours. She had a talent of seeing people's incarnations. When we meditated across each other, she would focus and tell me the figures she sees in front of me. She was another friend that I was able to share my clairvoyance and experiences with numbers.

That summer she got sick so that she needed to stay in the hospital for two months. It was very hard for me to be away from her. I prayed and sent love and light to her. I would write to her every day whether she replied me or not. I told her about the crows and hearing their caws as a good symbol. I told her that I knew she would feel better soon and come back home. Doctors did not allow her to use Internet, make phone calls or have visitors. I had to be patient. Sometimes she was able to use her computer. During that time, I started to see crows more often and asked them to help my friend.

One afternoon I was checking my emails, hoping to hear from my friend and saw that I had one new mail waiting for me. It was from her. She was telling me that she was feeling better. Her room was seeing the garden of the hospital that she was watching the crows every morning. She said they were such wonderful birds as I said. Reading that I was communicating with them made her so excited that she felt stronger every time she saw them. I was so touched by her email. So thankful that crows were healing my friend. I wished that the crows that were flying in my garden were the ones flying in her garden. I sent her energy with the help of crows.

So than time passed easier for both of us.

Nature as my inspiration

The more I believed in nature, the more I cherished my life. I became more grounded and lively. I felt the energy of life floating within me. Nothing more than receiving and sending love would have made me happier. I had love all around me. I only needed to feel the Divine love that was always available to me in all ways through my senses. Sending me light and guidance. My heart was peaceful with what I was experiencing all the time. I was heartbroken but I knew that time would heal everything. Taking long hours of walk in the park, watching the birds and the trees, looking into their shimmering light to see the crystal sparks in beautiful flowers has helped me to move on.

Lights that shine on the sea had a healing effect. Sometimes I would take the boat to travel on the Bosporus. Sea gulls flying over the boat and near it were always bringing joy to my soul. Princess islands were an escape from all the rush and noise of the city. Travelling by the sea to reach the islands was exciting. Salesmen on the boat would bring all kinds of different objects that you would not find easily somewhere else and show them excitingly to the passengers. Their way of explaining the products would lock many travelers attention. They would listen him as if they were listening a storyteller. Container ships passing along the way moving in slow motion with the heaviness, carrying colorful boxes filled with materials from all around the world. Maybe carrying the products that the salesman was trying to sell us on the boat that I was travelling on. Maybe just passing from Bosporus to reach the destination on the east. All different kinds of people were travelling on the same boat aiming to reach the same direction. Looking at the far distances of the sea. All have faces that carry different thoughts and stories. Some are angry looking, some tired and some careless but most of them sad.

My inner self was always longing for connection. Every each animal was singing a lullaby for my defenses to fall asleep. The smell of earth, the detoxification of the mud, the coldness of each drop of rain and the touch of wind was all that I needed. Rocks that I rested on, the trees that I laid my back or hugged and the grass I stepped on were all telling me a fairy tale. No matter what was going on in my life, they were helping me to see the good side. They were the angels on earth.

Princess Island has a big natural park for the visitors to walk and enjoy the high pine trees. Old high pine trees were always hiding the squirrels and little singing birds for the eyes to catch and laugh. Horse carriages travelling around the island would help the visitors to travel around. Smelling the horses and hearing horseshoes sound hitting on the ground made me travel back and forth in time. The church on top of the island has a wonderful view of the island and the forest. When you reach the end of the hill, you are only allowed to travel on foot to see the church. Travelling to the end of the hill is very joyful when you pass through beautiful summerhouses and enjoy their gardens with angel statues.

You would feel like angels are guiding you to reach the church. Than you would come to the hill and you would see rabbits painted in pink waiting in boxes of gypsies for the visitors to pet them and ask for a wish. Gypsies would look into the eyes, pet the rabbit and let the pink rabbit point a piece of paper with the fortune. Young girls would gather in front of the rabbits to see their fortune with faith. Than the long travel to walk on top of the hill would start. The legend says that if you keep your silence, never look back and chose to take your shoes off than your wish would come true when you reach to the church.

Well you would start walking and hear the voices of the forest talking to you. Little fountains to drink water would steam next to the wide path. You would see papers hanged on the trees with wishes written inside and cautions for people to respect the trees and not to hang any more papers. Sea is looking at you time to time between the pine trees. It would take ten to fifteen minutes to reach the top of the hill but it would feel more or less like it.

I would start murmuring my prayers all along the way. Thinking of the positive affirmations and dreaming on a beautiful future ahead of me all along the way would always let me reach the church sooner than I expected. Warmed face welcomes would greet me when I reached the peaceful atmosphere of the church. I would walk a small narrow pathway to come to the entrance than wear a robe as a sign of respect to the church. Priests would greet you in the entrance and you would hear the rituals with a mystical atmosphere of the sacred candles. All the icons, plates of the angels, Mother Mary statues and Jesus paintings are hanged on the walls. Some left their canes in the church as a sign of health they received after their visit. After prayers were sent to God and father's blessings were received, I would write down my affirmations or wishes on a piece of paper and leave it in the box of the church as requested.

CHAPTER VII

Beauty in light

When I needed a wake-up call, Universe was sending it to me through nature. Flowers in my house were communicating with me. They were blossoming when I was cheerful. They would lean to the side when I needed more attention in my life. The music that was playing in my house was singing to their roots. Their leaves were shaking when I was singing to them. The smell in their blossom was awakening my instincts every time I sniffed them with my gratitude. My inner voice was telling me to touch their soil every morning. Hear their call for energy and love.

Placing my crystals to their soil was an exchange of energy between them and me. Universe was all about sending and receiving. There is a great balance in the recycle of love. Universe is always there for us when we need it. Loneliness is just a phase created for strengthening our ego. When we looked around there is always piece of love in all, light and energy within every soul of human, animal, nature, and object. All we need to do is ask for the call and receive it when it comes. It will always come in a form you asked for in need. Sometimes mended in a different form but always in the form that is best for our own good. Just being open to our senses and to the spirit carried the beauty into my life.

Some would see beauty in a person, some in object and some would see it in nature. They are all one to me even the ugliness has the beauties inside itself according to me. The gaze of the viewer makes the presence beautiful or ugly. We all live in an illusion of the mind on the three dimensional world. Our fears and hopes are the guidelines to create the life we ask in return. Self-acceptance, respect, love and gratitude through seeing all the capabilities we have are the key to a happier life. Abundance is all around us depending on what we want from life. Accepting the past in peace, seeing the present in love and looking at future in faith is the key as a Tibetan monk once said to my friend. Our prayers coming from the heart would guide us to this beauty. Living the moment with the joy of living and accepting the present only helps us all to be in oneness.

Good or bad, beautiful or ugly, right or wrong, and opposite or negative all unites in one. We all need them at the end to be able to see the creation. All opposites teach us something that we need them both. Good and evil are all guidelines and growth lessons in life. There is only innocence in people depending on what is experienced. We should not fight with opposites and block the energy but let it show us the way. Only barrier that we built to ourselves is not to see the light in both sides. Darkness is also a positive thing when you learn to look for the light within it. Darkness is good when you accept it as it is.

All the growth lessons are there to teach us to live a better life. We all need to find peace within ourselves so that we would live healthier. If we do not see evil than how could we differentiate the goodness? We all need them at the end to walk the path to light. Light only means being in peace and carrying on the brightness and lightness of letting life go, as it needs to be. We need to learn to accept life in order to see the possibilities. Possibility of beauty in everything is the potential of life. Unconditional love is to see the possibility and letting it to find its own path. One day everything would find its way whether we live to see it or not but knowing that soul and spirit will see it in one passing time is the challenge of life.

Challenges are given to us not to struggle with them. Challenges are there for us to learn through them. Struggle is good when you live it in a happy way. Struggle is not well for your health if you choose to live it in a stressful manner by not following your heart. When the voice within starts to die than you need to slow down. Voice is always the guideline and the good feeling inside is our fuel. When you receive pain inside than it means that you had shot the doors to the light of opportunities. Even that pain is speaking that would be a sign that there is something craving within to come out.

All you need to do is to stop and accept the high potential in nothing. Nothing is something. Good is bad so the bad is good. Nothing is something so does the opposite. When you let yourself listen to nothing you would hear something. Whether you hear it in a good or bad way, it will teach you something. That is beauty whether it is ugly or not. Accept being as it is.

Thee who follow self would find special gifts within filled with surprises.

Unity

Gifts are the meaning of life and learning to be happy. Meaning of life is there to understand oneness in all. We are all interconnected. All you need to do is call for the one, invite one into your life and one day when you least expect it; it would knock on your door for you to welcome. Once you learn to trust life and be brave in your actions in order to embrace it, than all that you need would come in abundance. You might think that you just need a little but Universe would always give you more than you asked for. Abundance is in the form of happiness. Material life would not feed you well but the spiritual life would always bring wealth. Spiritually living in order to appreciate all in once is the essence of life. Simplicity is the richness of life.

That is all nature and spirit was teaching me. Everyday it was making me dizzy when I add a line to it. It was all running within me. All these information was coming in front of me through the people I met or readings I found. My mind was interpreting the information and reminding me that I knew all that when I was born. It was in my Akasha. All I needed was to be open to it than that it would be present to me. My soul would walk the path with me and direct me to all the information that I needed. If I was not careful enough than a person would cut the line in front of me by pointing the book I needed to see. All I needed was to pay attention to the signs that life is offering. I just should not fight anything in the traffic of life but try to see the hidden message behind. They were all there for a reason. There were endless opportunities. I was never early or late for anything. Even if I miss one at once than a better one or the same one would be presented to me when the divine timing comes.

Me only wanted to be me and it was showing me the path to find it within me.

CHAPTER VIII

Strength of the dragon

2011 was the year of the rabbit. I did not know about the Chinese horoscope until one day I saw a Chinese calendar in a shop with a cute rabbit drawing on. I asked the shop owner what it was and she explained me the meaning behind the calendar. That year I started to draw rabbits for luck. At the end of the rabbit year, we entered the Dragon year, which was around November. I was interested with rabbits and their fury coat and funny face that I was delighted to paint rabbits.

When my exhibition was done most of my paintings were with rabbits. I even painted healing snakes with rabbit heads. At the show's opening, I met a yoga teacher. She was a very interesting woman with a deep spiritual interest and knowledge. The paintings and the poems took her interest so that she wanted to meet me and talk about them in depth. She asked me what my Chinese horoscope sign. I told her that it was the hen. She told me that my year was coming, which was the year of the dragon. She told me to drop on focusing into rabbits and instead seek my strength in the dragon. Rabbits were for luck for sure and wise in their speed but unless you were strong you would not reach any goal. She said everyone would fear the dragon but not the hen but when they come together they would bring luck and strength. She told me to put a dragon sign on my side or wear it on me. She warned me that the dragon was inside of every hen in order to find it I was suppose to choose to face it.

So I nod and smiled. People around us dazzled with our conversation. They did not understand a word but saw that we spoke the same language of the spirit. She was there to awaken something in me that I did not know at that time.

After the opening, I never saw her again. I tried to find her contact but I could not. It was a sign given to me so that I chose to direct my attention to dragons. Surprisingly a week later my mother brought me a dragon necklace for luck as a gift. She told me that she found out that it was the Dragon year so she got it for me for luck. My mother was always there for me when I needed her. She had invisible eyes and ears working on me. She said the dragon's strength would be there to protect me.

In many Western cultures, Dragons were a symbol for fear as a beast that attacks knights. However, in Chinese mythology it was used for strength and good luck. In Japanese culture, Quan Yin was carried on a dragon. She was the symbol for compassion and love. I searched on the various meanings of the dragon. In that summer, I attended a business meeting in United States with my father. All the Chinese and Tai restaurants had the pictures of dragons at their doors. I took photos of them. I decided to use them in my paintings. I knew that it would bring me new insight and knowledge.

My life was getting more meaningful in a spiritual manner that my work started to reflect it more in a positive manner. I started to become more concerned about my well being by becoming a better person in order to reflect more positive messages in my work. I had a purpose of clearing my past and stepping into a new life. In order to do it, I was trying to open myself more to love by focusing on my heart chakra. In my meditations, I was concentrating on healing my heart and opening myself more to love by believing that love was all around me. I was reminding myself that I was loved and loveable. Dedicating myself more to meanings of signs and symbols has helped me to visualize them more.

I started to use the symbols as they appeared in my conscious mind instead of the ones I found in the books. I was only aiming to heal my present situations and presenting the methods of healing I found. I started to follow my heart and only using my instincts. It was like being more creative by connecting to a higher self. So that instead of me loading information to the paintings, my work started to seem like trying to give me a message. It was as if I was learning through my paintings. I started to work extra hours. I was painting with extra joy that it became a tool for me to heal and forget my grief or weaknesses. I knew that I would understand it when the right timing comes.

In that period of my life, I had a successful exhibition and had already started to work on my upcoming show for the next year. I should have been happy with what I had but instead I was very heartbroken and devastated. I needed to make my decision to move to a new apartment and start to make a new life. I believed a change of place would bring in new energies. I needed to let the past behind and move into a new place and start a new page. I was feeling hopeless and weak. I was seeing an open door for me but not having the strength to step into it. My trouble was being afraid of change. The extra hours of working was keeping me away from fear. I only needed to have the patience to understand and see the messages hidden behind. The work of the spirit was an endless road. Every time I thought I was done, I realized I was just starting.

Changes in life style

I started by changing my life style. I started to exercise and eat healthier. I was working a lot still but looking for ways to be stronger and more energetic. It was a perfect time to take a chance on a new beginning. I was feeling very tired from working. My whole body was hurting and was not able to work any longer. I felt that my body was giving me the signal to give a break. So I decided to spend more time with friends and follow my inner voice to start a healthier life by exercising.

One day I had a coffee with a really good friend of mine. She said she had just started working with a personal fitness coach. She was having very good results by eating healthier and feeling stronger. That is what I needed at that time so I asked her to give me his name and number to call. I saved the number and put a picture of a dragon photo in order to remember what it was for.

I was ready to find the dragon within me. I called the trainer and had an appointment with him for the next week. I thought making a choice and starting to commit on it was the best decision I have ever done. I knew that there was something wrong with me as long as I was not able to paint as much as I used to and feeling weak than I had to find a person to direct me into the right direction.

I was eating very unhealthy at that time and my sleeping hours were very unbalanced. Unfortunately I had trouble of sleeping at night because I had high heart rates and was feeling very hyper at nights. I never questioned the reason but thought it was normal as long as I was eating unhealthy. I always had a reason or an excuse for every kind of problem I had. I never thought that I was unhealthy because I thought I was the healthiest person and nothing could ever happen to me.

It was time to start exercising and face the demons, the fear I had for sports.

CHAPTER IX

Meeting the dragon

Tony Hill was my personal fitness coach. We worked for two moths and the results were extra ordinary for me. He was watching me closely and monitoring my exercises. He cautioned me from the first day that he had every tool for the first aid just in case something goes wrong. So he was very conscious of what he was doing that in return I trusted him. He motivated me and worked out with me to change my life style from my eating habits to exercising hours.

My sleeping hours went back to normal after working out three days a week with him. I was also doing the home exercises he was asking me to do. Through time I was able to complete the given home works. I was only able to do one hundred crunches and ended up doing five hundred with no difficulty. I was walking half an hour to his office and getting started as soon as I enter his work out room. He was greeting me with his wonderful big bright happy smile.

Tony is a wonderful person with a great spiritual sight and joyful heart. He knew what he was doing and enjoying it. My achievements were making him proud that I could see his eyes shining brighter when I completed a set of exercises. He had the technology all around. He was arranging his ipad for work out minutes than would clap his hands for me to finish it on time.

Tony was working with his wonderful family. He and his wife Karen Hill were running the Burning Fitness Center. Karen was responsible with the nutrition of the customers and Tony was the fitness coach. Karen had a holistic nutrition that she had her own style for teaching her customers good living. She encouraged for eating organic food and always had a positive attitude. They were both very responsible with their followers I would say. The reason is that when you choose to follow their style for good living than they fed your body and soul. I was lucky to come across them through my life.

Karen and Tony came to Istanbul two years before I met them. Their mission was to show Turkish community a healthy life style by giving them the great tips to exercise and eat well. So they were not asking for people to do diet but asking them to choose the right food. In order to be able to complete their program, you should choose to live a healthy life style. They encouraged their followers to stop smoking, drinking, eating junk food and instead processing food that is giving you energy. They were giving seminars all around. They also prepared exercising DVDs that would encourage people, families, handicaps, children and even military boot camps with their wonderful techniques and nutrition facts. They were only about helping people to live better lives.

I was a good follower. Tony found my figure well and told me to only build muscles and follow the food program he would send me. Therefore, I did a fifteen days detox without milk, cheese, eggs and meat. I was a vegetarian for fifteen days. At the beginning it was very hard to follow as a person with a history of eating hamburgers, drinking caffeine, having a glass of alcohol at least twice a week but through time I started to feel better. I was fresh and renewed. My first month I was feeling tired but had a sense of breathing and tasting the food I eat much better. I was getting stronger. My muscles were growing that I started to walk straight and I became a size smaller. I was not aiming to look thinner but becoming fit and strong that I would be able to paint as fast as I used to. I was always feeling tired, sleepy, and breathless but was not able to sleep well that I was planning to fix it with Tony.

However after one month of exercise I started to get worse. I should have felt much more energetic through time like the rest of the people but I started to feel weaker. Tony was sensing something unusual with me but was not sure.

So my muscles were built that I should have felt stronger, but instead I was feeling weaker by feeling much more tired. I started to feel an extra-ordinary pain on my back and shoulders but was not able to explain it. I thought it was the way to build some muscles that I should feel some pain. I decided to push my self more and more. I started to wake up six in the morning, walk my two dogs, get my quick breakfast and walk half an hour to the fitness center, exercise for half an hour and walk back to my place. I was feeling fine at the beginning. I even started to look better but my energy level was not rising. One day I realized that I started to breathe harder, sweat very quickly and feel drowsy. I found it abnormal.

One day I was not able to walk to the fitness center. I felt breathless in the middle of the way, stopped walking, and put my hand on my panting heart. It was moving as if it was going to come out of my chest. I walked slowly and by the time I arrived at the fitness center, I was feeling dizzy. I was not sure what was going on with my body. I thought I needed to work out in order to be fit like others. I thought I was only feeling sleepy and lazy.

I took a small break after my arrival and than went on top of the fitness machine to start my usual routine. Five minutes later, I was feeling breathless and was so much in pain, became all red and was hardly speaking. I pushed the stop sign and gave the emergency signal. Tony told me to stop as soon as he saw me. He said it was very unusual for me to still feel tired after two month of exercising. He took my wrist to check my heart rate. The result was not usual so that he told me to stop for the day and see a doctor.

As thirty-two years old I had never been to a cardiologist. I never thought of calling one for an appointment or even stepping into their office. I had some problems but it was always related to my low-blood sugar, low blood rate or thyroids. After working on my crystals and meditating regularly, my health was constantly getting better. Through years my eyesight problem healed and my thyroids disappeared by meditating. All this healing was a surprise for my doctors but not to me. I always believed in my self and my ability to cure my self. I knew that all was in my mind. I was certain of my self and my body. I thought I was very healthy until my visit to see a cardiologist.

CHAPTER X

Visit to my grandmother's Cardiologist

When I went for a visit to my parent's house for the weekend, I realized that my troubles were worse. I had difficulty going from my room at the basement floor to my parent's room on the third floor, approximately thirty steps, became a burden for me. I decided to tell this to my mother. She asked me to try to go up the stairs in the next morning and after listening to my heart, she was surprised. She said she found it unusual as well that she decided to ask for an appointment from my grandmother's cardiologist. I found it unusual as long as I had never had a full check-up in my life. I told her that every thing would be fine but she looked worried. She insisted on coming to the doctor with me. After long hours of discussion, she ended up in the car next to me to head for the doctor.

The doctor's office had a big waiting room with lots of visitors waiting on him. All of them were elder people accept a young woman sitting silently by reading a book. I was glad that there was at least one patient around my age waiting to see the doctor but later I found out that she was waiting on for her father to come out of the doctor's office. When my name was called, I went into the doctor's directed room, which was a dark old office.

The doctor was a lean, tall, old man with a welcoming face. He was also confused with the patient by assuming that my mother was there to see him. After finding out that I was the one with the appointment. He asked me to explain my circumstances for visiting him. So I began explaining him my situation, answered couple of his questions and showed him my blood tests that were asked. He looked at them and found my results very appealing. I was a non-smoker, regularly exercising and a social drinker once or twice a month. They were all very healthy and good manners to him. He praised me with my life choices and asked me to go to the next room.

The next room was bigger with lots of screens and a treadmill with lots of cables. He asked me to lie on the bed next to the MRI, magnetic resonance imaging to screen my heart. I wore the special dress they gave me and laid on the bed on the cold dark room. The doctor entered the room, sat the stool beside the bed. He asked me to turn my back and lay on my left side so that he can easily reach my heart. Afterwards he squeezed some gel on my chest for the machine to slide. Later he started to scan my chest and look at his screen to examine.

There was a long silence. I was hardly thinking anything but listening to my heart's beat coming from the machine. It took him very long. He said he was sorry for the long wait and thanked me for my patience. I was not aware how long it took him but I suspected that it was unusually long. So I told him that I might be psychologically depressed that I might be feeling panic attacks but I was seeing a psychologist for almost ten years and she was finding me very good. I had some difficulties in the chest but I told him that they were all psychological. I thought he was just trying to find something wrong on a healthy body that I was trying to excuse my self by listing excuses. He did not choose to reply as I thought he would but instead asked me to keep my silence for more. At that instant I figured out that something was not right.

He inhaled deeply and asked me to turn. Then he looked into my eyes with an anxious face. He was looking worried not like the time I met him. He started to praise me with many compliments that I thought a negative speech was coming close. He said:

"You are a very good-natured and calm person Sezin that there is nothing wrong with your psychology as your psychologist told you. However your heart is not healthy that it is giving you all the troubles you had. You are not depressed or heartbroken or troubled but unhealthy. I saw it here on the screen but had to be hundred percent sure that I took my time. I see a tumor in your heart. Well before explaining to you, ı would prefer to talk to your mother. She is very right to be worried and very good that she came here with you."

I was very surprised and could not understand what he meant. He suddenly left the room without a word. I started to wait on them to come back. I was very sure that I was fine that I was not able to make sense of his behavior. I did not understand the meaning of tumor. I even was not sure that I heard him right. I waited on for a long time for them to get back. I started to breathe deeply that I could let go of everything and start this thing over. I waited for them by breathing and finally they came in. When they did, my mother was not looking well but pretending to be smiling. At that instant I felt lost.

The big entry

The doctor entered into the room with my mother. My mother was looking much more worried than before. They both started to talk together or maybe I thought they were because my ears were blocked. I was not sure what their conversation was about. It was like they were talking in a different language. I only felt my ears ringing from panic and surprise. Doctor's assistant entered in the room as well five minutes after their big entry.

Everyone was looking sad and worried now. The room's atmosphere became darker as if someone chose to put the lights down without telling anyone. They were all staring at the MRI screen. The black screen was covered with fingerprints from pointing out different parts of my black and white heart. I was not sure what they were seeing in there. I was not interested with it. I only wanted to leave that small, claustrophobic, airless and dark room.

I was not sure how the atmosphere of a room could have changed this much in an instant.

I finally had the courage to ask them what was wrong with me. Doctor said I had a tumor located in the left atrium of my heart probably since birth. It was called Myxoma. He said it was a rare symptom but nothing to be afraid of as long as the tumor was not stuck to the inside layer of the heart but instead choosing to hang down. These kinds of tumors were treatable and were not risky. They were easily removed. It was a rare symptom and all the patients would have tremendous difficulties that he was surprised that I did not realize it before. He found its size not too small but also not too big.

I asked him what we would do about it. He looked at me with a pity in his eyes but was not able to put the words together. I asked him if it would go away with taking medicine. He said I would need to get a surgery to remove it. He said it was not large and was not looking dangerous as long as it was hanging down like a broccoli. He explained that if it would be stuck to the wall of the heart than it would be bad natured. At that instant I found out that the tumor I had might carry the risk of cancer. I thanked God that it was hanging down. My tumor was good-natured, whatever that meant. He started to give the full explanation, risks, and all the good chances I had for a long time. I was just daydreaming. I did not want to be in that room but somewhere else with silence.

The doctor explained that at some point with giving extra effort the tumor was obscuring the normal flow of the blood within the chambers of the heart so that the patients were regularly fainting. The worse scenario was tumor growing to an extend size which would lead to death. This kind of tumor was generally found on women. Many patients that have not realized their problem have died when giving birth.

Finally, after thirty years I found out the reason behind my chest pains, difficulty of breathing, hearing my heartbeat, dark circles underneath my eyes, diarias, long PMS, long difficult periods and swollen feet. They were all the symptoms of Myxoma, my broccoli. I was not weak. I was not lazy. I was not a coward. I was not depressed or addicted to anger. I was never aggravating my pain. All my problems were because of a broccoli shaped tumor.

Huge change in my life was waiting on me.

CHAPTER XI

Broccoli Shaped Tumor

I looked at my doctor and my mother and did not know what they were talking about. They told me that it would be a small and quick operation so I chose to believe in them. I did not ask the aftermath or the process. I felt like a fool. I chose to become a fool. I became a great example of three monkeys. I was not hearing, talking or seeing anything properly. I chose to become three monkeys for my own peace and harmony. I always thought it would be bad to ignore things but at that moment acceptance led me to ignorance with consciousness.

Divine timing was perfect because heart surgeries were easier than before today. They had Da Vinci Robot, which was making three little holes on your chest next to your breast and getting inside to suck the tumor out of your system. Da Vinci was an artistic name so it sounded good to me. Ten years of psychological therapy worth something at that moment, I realized I was calm and accepting the situation with peace. All my meditations that I had done in the last five years were more meaningful to me than before. Everything made sense to me. First time in my life I understood the meaning of divine timing and my life purpose. My existence had a meaning more than I had imagined. God gave me another chance to live and see the value of my life.

I thought of the last chapters of my life. I reviewed all the things I had learned in the past couple of years in couple of minutes in that doctor's office. All the scenes slipped through my mind in a second like a fast-forwarding movie scene. All things were not a coincidence but made to be just to prepare me to that chosen moment, which will give me a new consciousness to understand the meaning of my existence. This tumor was there from the first day I was born. I was meant to have a surgery from the first day I came to this earth but its timing was very important. If I had a full check up before than the doctors would have found out about the tumor years ago but than I would have a much more difficult surgery without the technology of today. On the other hand, if my working has not pushed me hard to find a way to exercise than I would not be able to meet my personal fitness trainer who figured out my problem. When I thought about those things, I come to a conclusion of the 6 degrees of life that lead me to find my doctor. If we go back and rewind the story of me than we could easily find the miraculous connection.

When I first moved to my apartment, I chose to give a break to go to Paris. I met a man called Gabrielle at a restaurant. He presented his card to me so did I. He liked my paintings so I liked his bags that he designed.

So we became friends. He introduced his friends to me. So one of them became my best friend called Sahar. She introduced me to Tony Hill who became my personal fitness coach. Tony had recently moved to Turkey. My friend Sahar had also recently moved to Istanbul from Paris. Tony came all the way from California to Istanbul. I met Gabrielle all the way in Paris to meet these three people that led me to go to a cardiologist who led me to the best doctor in Istanbul. Life is a miracle itself. We all came to this world with a reason to help one another. All was for a good reason. Even my ex-boyfriend had a reason to enter into my life. He thought me to be patient, strong and accept everything as it was.

I breathed in and exhaled. Breathed in and exhaled. Breathed in and exhaled. Closed my eyes. I chose to enjoy the moment no matter what was going on. I surrendered and let go... At that exact moment, everything looked to me like a movie scene.

When I woke up from daydreaming back to the large MRI room in the cardiologist's office. I turned and looked at the screen that everyone was looking at and started to laugh. They turned and looked at me with a surprise. All that I could tell them was:

- I am happy that you would not give me an effort test. I forgot to bring an extra t-shirt. The broccoli is really hanging down from there. Is not it?

Exquisite.
Maybe that was bliss.

CHAPTER XII

Good luck in the Hospital

A day before going to the hospital, I prayed for a sign and prayed for many signs to guide me during my stay in the hospital. I had never had a surgery or been in hospital for more than couple of hours. So this was all new for me.

I was packing my goods to a small suitcase and a big shoulder bag. While I was doing so, I was praying with deep meditation. Than suddenly at the end of my big pink bag I felt something. My Bahia charms, which were lost for a year, came out just at the end of that big bag. I had not seen or used it for a long time. They were totally lost. I did not pack for travel for a long time that I had forgot it in my travel bag. Now Bahia charms, my lucky charms, are a gift from my mother from Brazil. Brazilians believed in and prayed for The Goddess Yemenja and carried her charms as a protector. She is believed to bring good luck by bringing new opportunities. The charms are represented with colorful ropes hanging down from a chain. My mother visited a church in Brazil and got the

Bahia charms for me for my protection and luck. Yemenja is the Goddess of the sea and protector of the lovely shores of Brazil. I knew at that moment that angels were with me by answering my prayers. I felt their care and warmth of love all surrounding me. I asked for a sign and they sent it to me in order to prove their existence. They said they were with me.

Bahia was telling me that all doors for great beginnings were opening for me. I have been afraid for too long to enter into new doors but now I was able to accept all as good. Everything was in order and under control. I was filled with faith and trust. I took a deep breath and exhaled all my worries for my angels to wash away and clean. Than left home for my great journey. I knew that I was watched over and protected.

Support

I had difficulties to express myself, a specially asking for something in need. All I needed during this time was support and love from God, angels, family and friends. I did not know how to ask in a proper manner. I thought it would be a bother or that I would sound as complaining.

I was always told to stand on my own feet and never show my weakness or grief. I was always thought to look strong and never in need. However, I asked for my angels' guiding hand in this situation. They were strongly telling me to ask for help from friends and family. I was strongly hearing the urge within me to share my difficult time with my friends. I felt that I needed the support. It was time for me to change by leaving all the manners I learned in the past.

I decided to give a big notice to everyone by mail about my surgery. It was a very difficult task for me but what would I loose. So I believed that there was a surprise for me in deed. I posted on the net that I was leaving home for hospital. I emailed all the friends even my ex-boyfriend whom was not talking to me. I text messaged all my friends. I called my best friend, Leyla from childhood, to bring me good luck slippers for my hospital stay. I called my other best friend, Yasemin to be there for me before my surgery.

Prayed God that I would not get disappointed at least in the hospital. I let go and let my prayers be in charge. I did not hear back from some of my friends but I let go.

I first received Leyla's gift, which were rabbit shaped slippers in white as I asked from her. It was a sign that things would go smooth and easy. She knew that I loved rabbits so she picked my favorites. Afterwards the phone calls and messages came following one after another. Everybody was trying to be there for me. My best friend Evrim, living in another city, called my mother and me every day before my surgery. He called my mother during the surgery for support. They were all there to motivate my family and me. I was surprised and happy on the other end too. It was like a quest showing me that I was loved and lovable. All I needed to do was allow the process by being open. It motivated me and helped me to feel grateful.

<u>Departure</u>

On Monday, I left my house early in the morning. All during the way my parents were silent. We were all watching out of our own windows. I was looking around as if I was looking at them the first time. All looked different to me. I was asleep but awake at the same time. I was just watching around and daydreaming. People kept calling my parents. Nobody was able to talk to me. I was in deep shock. I was afraid but not aware of it. I did not know what was going to happen. I was not questioning it. I was not listening to the answers. I was just letting the happenings take me over. I was repeating myself that all that was happening was happening for my highest good.

We arrived to the hospital. Escalator took us to the third floor where the heart patients were staying. It was a corridor that was secluded, sanitized and silent. There were special nurses waiting on the corridor. We entered to a room given to us. It had a bed and a sofa. I did not like something about the room. It just did not feel right to me. Maybe I did not get the vibes. My mother was worried that we would need to stay in that room. It was too hot for her. I told her to wait cause I felt that the room would change. She laughed cause it seemed impossible to her.

The room number was not giving me the right vibrations. Suddenly the nurse entered in and told us that we would need to change to room 227. I said to myself that good thinking would bring me miracles. The new room was telling me to stay positive to ensure that I was safe with my angels. As soon as I made myself believe in the power of seven, I felt strong. 227 meant good thinking would bring on the great miracles and surround you with the right people. When we stepped in the new room I felt good. My mother was also happy. I felt like everything was changing in a good manner. Signs were following me around with the help of my guiding angels.

Many sweet nurtured nurses started to enter into the new room. I was smiling at them and their expressions were turning into laughter and happiness. I suddenly felt lucky that I was able to control my feelings and see things in a miraculous manner. I had all the tests before the surgery. I had to stay a day in the hospital on the date of my lovely ex-boyfriend's birthday. I was trying to forget the grief of not hearing from him and also trying to forget the anxiety of the surgery. God helped me in my decision. Many friends came to visit me. They brought me teddy bears and candies. My mothers best friend Lidya brought me Mother Mary icon to protect me and bring me peace. I placed all of them beside my bed. I asked for balloons and my aunt sent me dozens of them in many different colors.

At the end of the day, the room 227 became colorful and bright. I was trying to make myself believe that I would be going to give birth on the 20th of November. Birth to a new, clean, bright, and loving heart that knows how to bring happiness into my precious soul. When doctors entered in to explain me the surgery, I just chose to daydream. I let myself ignore their surprise when they found out that it was me who was there for the surgery. I closed my ears when they told me that I was too young for a heart surgery. I just told myself that I was lucky to be alive. I was just lucky that my poor heart had let me live up to that day and would let me live better in the coming years.

The midnight came and I was still awake. I could only hear the screams of a woman next door. She was out of her surgery and screaming out of pain. She was screaming for painkillers. I realized that I was afraid. I told to myself that everything would just be fine. I breathe in and out calmly and imagined myself on top of pink clouds. I dreamed of the screams as dolphins and horses screams. I dreamed myself flying on top of pink clouds with colorful unicorns. Through dreaming, I put myself into sleep and suddenly without notice I felt asleep.

Day of the surgery

The next morning a nurse was calling my name to wake me up at six am. I saw two of my friends, Yasemin and Tanla, waiting for me to wake up. They were there for me to wish me luck. One of them was beautifully dressed in orange only for me to feel energetic. She said that she was there for me as a rising sun. I smiled at her and felt that the sun was rising in my self. I thanked them. My best friend Yasemin was looking into my eyes with support and courage. They chose to come to visit me before they go to work. I knew that I was not alone.

Some of my mother's friends came into the room and gave me their prayers. I was surrounded with beautiful people. I asked for my mother to stay with me so she did stay. My father was not around much because he was not able to hide his feelings much so my mother asked him to be away. He was very worried and anxious. The room was filled with the morning light.

I remember that day very clearly. It had a different light. The atmosphere was mysterious and spooky. It was very silent and quiet that it was like a sceen from a movie. I had so many feelings running through my mind that I was not able to follow. I was not able to hear what my friends were telling me. I did not know what to do or say but just wait on the nurse to show up to put me to sleep.

The nurse put a shot on my back and suddenly everywhere became foggy. I just saw the four-leaved clover sign on top of my bed that would carry me to the surgery room. I screamed with happiness.

I do not remember the rest but my mother told me the rest of the story. I screamed out that I was so lucky that clover was there for me as a sign. My friends were laughing. I was only laughing, asking everyone staying on the corridor to come to party with me. I was asking my mother to come and join me. I was telling everyone that I was leaving for a party. So people came out of their rooms with surprise.

They waved goodbye and sent their prayers to my mother and me.

So I was a sleep…

CHAPTER XIII

Intensive Care Unit

All was in white and I heard some noises that I could not recall. My eyes were open and evaluating its surrounding. There were no windows to see outside or understand the time. Suddenly I found a clock hanging on the wall right in front of me. It said four. I was not sure if it was in the morning or in the afternoon. It was not indicating pm or am. I realized I was in a room filled with people rushing around but did not know what they were doing. I was not sure how I got in there. I tried to move but realized I was numb. Half of my body was not sensing anything and the other half was all in a terrible pain. I could never define my pain but this felt like being toasted in between two heavy hot bars.

Next, I sensed my dry mouth. I felt like I was not able to swallow. Suddenly I figured out that I was hardly breathing. It felt like there was no air. I sensed some tubes coming out of my neck. I heard some beepers around me. So many serum bottles were hanging around me. Some digital machines were around me. I could not recognize any of them. Nurses were running around to check on them. I felt a huge rock was sitting on top of my chest. So that I looked on my breasts but I saw nothing. I checked if there were thousands of knives stabbing my chest but there were none. I felt like a metal plate was stuck inside me. I was curious what was placed inside me. It was an undefined pain.

I looked around carefully and realized that the last thing I could remember was that I went to a surgery. I suddenly heard my slow voice. I was repeating the same two words unconsciously. First I heard 'Mother', second I heard the name of my ex-boyfriend coming out of my mouth silently. Suddenly, I felt too shamed of myself so sad. I stopped myself repeating his name. I could not believe my self that I was able to think of him unconsciously. He was someone that was never there for me and my poor heart was still carrying his burden. How could I still love him? I decided to stop thinking when a larger stabbing went into my heart. I realized I had to think only of good things.

A man came next to my bed. He said in an automatic tone:

"You just woke up in an intensive care room. Your surgery went very well. Let us know if you need anything."

I tried to open my mouth to ask for a glass of water but no voice was coming out. My voice was hardly coming out. I tried to breathe in to speak but it was too difficult. Probably I tried so hard that the man lean towards me to hear me. I felt like I was screaming but a small voice came out as:

"Water."

"Sorry but you are not allowed to drink water."

Unfortunately I was not allowed to drink water. What kind of a health facility was it? Were they trying to cure me or kill me? I turned and looked into their eyes with a begging manner.

"We could only give you some ice cubes."

So they stuck ice cubes into my mouth. I was hardly holding them in my mouth. I was not able to control my mouth. It felt numb. They were only ice cubes but they felt miraclous. They were the best ice cubes I had in my life. I felt as if a waterfall was placed in my mouth.

Nurses were walking around me and holding some tubes, checking some machines, blood tubes and things that I had never seen before. I felt like an alien. My ice cube quickly melted in my mouth. Maybe time was too slow in that room. Maybe the ice cubes were smaller than I felt. Their slow movements in my mouth felt like I had never had something in my mouth cause the feeling of my body was extremely different. I was like I was not in my body accept the pain that I felt.

As I finished sucking the ice cubes, I started to realize the trouble; the pain was growing more and more. I was swearing to myself that I would never call anything pain after I come out of that room. The pain was like a tornado moving in my system. I felt the cramps in the stomach moving up towards my neck. I wanted to crumble and become small but was not able to move a muscle. I realized my stomach did not accept the ice cube.

I needed to throw up. I was always afraid to throw up and at that moment with that much pain I needed to throw up. My eyes widened up because of the pain I felt in my stomach. I realized I was really going to throw up. There was no escape. I understood at that instant why they did not want to give me a glass of water. I should have listened to them. I tried to catch their eye to let them know.

The nurses were extremely professional that they understood me in a minute. Than with a surprise they started to scream the word 'Liver'. I could not recall what they were talking. I got into panic. I was afraid that they would take my liver out. They ran around and one of them came with a liver.

I understood when they brought me the liver, which was the name of the metal liver shaped tray that I would need to throw into. What a name to give to a tray! A specially in a hospital! I suddenly forgot all the pain when I found out what the liver meant to the nurses. Terrible pain was rolling in my stomach and moving up to my chest towards my neck. All the water that I had hardly sucked and drank was now in the cup in a minute.

Suddenly I was thirsty again. I kept asking for water and had ice cubes and later threw in the liver. I do not know for how many times I did and how long this process took. Nurses were telling me to stop having ice cubes but I told to them that thirst was worse than the pain. They could not make sense but did what I asked them. They were surprised by my stubbornness. They brought me pillows and put on my side to ease my pain. I was feeling a big metal wheel placed on top of my heart. Everywhere was covered with bandages that I was not able to see what was hidden under my skin. All I wanted was to rip them of and ran out of that room.

Between consciousness and unconsciousness

I just wanted the time to pass quickly because I was awake earlier than I was supposed to. I was hearing the screams of the women laying next to my bed. They were both women. I was not able to understand one of them that I thought I forgot my own language as well. Then I thought I was able to understand the nurses. Nurses were asking for a translator. I figured out I was not the only one not able to understand her speech.

She was an Arabic woman who was asking for something but was not understood. I thanked God that I was not in her place. She was screaming so much that nurses were not able to hear me. I was just praying that she would stop. I had so much pain that I need painkillers. The nurses came and decided to give me the highest dose of morphine after long discussions. I felt dizzy. In a minute, I felt the rocks and knifes lifted, saw myself in a war fighting with troops. I was asking for help. Praying to find a paradise. I forced myself to think of the beach. I did but the troops came back. I wanted to cry but I could not. The pain was getting lesser and lesser. Pain was coming back and going away. Back and fort. I was trying to meditate but mixing all the mantras and prayers that I knew. Than, I felt like wetting my self. I felt drowsy and num. Finally I felt a sleep.

When I woke up, I saw the clock again it was 5:25 so that only an hour passed and minutes hands finally came on top of each other. I suddenly recalled what my grandmother thought me when I was a child.

"Your angels are with you when the hands of the hour and the minute come together on a clock. So you should make a wish."

I asked my angels for help. I was trying to recall all the prayers I knew. Suddenly I started to remember them slowly. I tried to say anything that came to my mind. I realized that my pain was getting lesser and lesser through prayer. I was so happy that my Higher Self was still with me. Nurses came near me and looked into my eyes and asked if I needed something. I only asked them to give me their hand and sent me my mother. She just looked into my eyes with a loving heart. I felt what she meant. She was not allowed to call my mother. I saw the sadness into her eyes.

I hold onto her soft hand very tight and did not let it go until I felt asleep.

My Nurse's Big Surprise

When I woke up I saw my mother standing next to my bed. I thought I was dreaming but as soon as I saw the nurse behind her; I realized that they called my mother into the room even if she was not allowed. I probably cried her name a lot in my dream.

My mother looked into my eyes deeply with a sadness and happiness blended without an expression but only loving affection. The room was dark. Probably it was late that everyone was put to sleep. There was only a small light behind my mother like a small desk light. It was giving her an affect like an angel coming out of darkness. I was only asking her through my eyes to save me from that cold dark room. It was good and safe to be in that room but it was also secluded and isolated. I was not alone but the fear moving through my body was making me feel alone.

The time before I saw my mother, I remember a nurse holding my arm and asking me to step out of the bed. I had a difficulty moving but he hold me strong and asked me to try. I said that I could not. He said if I could not than he would make me stay in intensive care room for one more day. I was going to burst out crying. I pleaded him not to allow that but instead help me to stand up. He held me strong and suddenly I found myself standing on the floor even if I had so much pain. He asked me to put a step forward. I looked at him defensively and did not say a word. He said all was right and helped me to get back to bed.

At that moment what hold me straight was the longing to see my mother and go back to the room 227. I needed to see the light. I needed to feel the warmth of the sun. I needed to see familiar faces and just be with my family. At that moment, I realized that I had everything in order to be happy.

I must have wished to see my mother so strongly that I could not believe in my eyes. I smiled at her with a surprise and she smiled back. I felt that she was holding herself strongly not to cry. She was a strong woman, a monument, a loving mother who was there for her one and only child. She was there for a support and she was sent by my angels. Nurses were my angels sent from heaven. I knew that they would be there for me since I saw the number 7 at my door the day before the surgery.

I was hardly holding my eyes open to see my mother. My eyes were falling down. I was forcing them to stay awake. I was too tried and the room was too dark. It was too hard for me to keep my curtains open. They were very heavy and weaving down to close. Probably it was late at night that they put the lights off. I kept thinking of the lights. My mind was uncontrolled. I tried to keep the image of my mother in my mind. She looked very different than her self that day. That five minutes visit felt like long hours to me. It made me feel stronger than I thought I was. Suddenly I lost control and went back to sleep. I held my mothers image in my mind like a souvenir from a space travel. I felt her hand in mine.

So my mother followed me through my dream.

The great cook

I don't remember how many times more I woke up and felt a sleep. I only remember waking up with the other patient's screams. She was probably known to be a great chef because she was asking for the nurses to let her go that she could check the food that she left at the stove. She was probably a good cook. The other Arabic woman was telling things that nobody was able to understand. God knows what she was talking about. Maybe she was concerned about her cooking abilities as well.

Who knows what the morphine could do to people? I was awaked with the name that I would not like to hear. What might I have screamed for before waking up? That is the secret of the nurses. Maybe I was begging the great chef to cook my ex like a cannibal.

The cook was trying to jump off the bed to save her last meal in her dreams. She was a very strong woman and probably very large in size. So I could trust her to cook whatever she wanted to cook. Nurses were shouting each other for help. They were calling up each other's name. Later they were trying to tie the great chef to bed. She was never tired of asking for her meal.

I was afraid to ask for painkillers. I only wanted to get out of that room. I felt as if I was in a nightmare that I wanted to wake up so badly but I could not. I was trying to meditate but I was not able to. I was trying to fall a sleep but the pain and the shouts did not let me. I still could not recall how I could be that much awake but not the others. Maybe they were brought there after me. I am not sure how I was that calm but not the others. I only knew that it must have been the faith that was holding me there.

The last time I woke up, nurses told me that it was time for me to leave. I smiled at them. I asked them about the cook. They could not make sense. They thought that I was another aware of my speech. I told them that I wanted to tell them a joke. They were surprised. I was hardly speaking but was trying to tell them a joke. They looked as if they got an electric shock. They probably wanted to laugh but they were just amazed that a patient in an intense care unit was trying to tell them a joke. However, they did not know that I only needed to hear some laughter. I knew that laughter was my best medicine. So I did tell them a short joke but they refused to laugh. Well I did.

Leaving for good

They grabbed me and put me in a different bed. I screamed out. They were afraid that they put me back to the old bed. They asked me what was wrong. I said I was afraid that I would fell. They laughed so hard that it put a smile on my face. I was so tiny compared to other patients that it was too easy for them to lift me. I should not be afraid but only let them carry me. It was sad that they were able to laugh at my fear but not at my jokes.

I surrendered and let it be and found myself in a new bed. They put a heart shaped pillow on my chest and told me to hold onto it very tight. Surprisingly it was letting my pain slip away every time I squeezed it to my chest. This one had wheels underneath it so that it was carrying me to the room 227. We went through long corridors. We passed in from of other intensive care units. When we were passing through small bumps, I was sticking onto the pillow not to feel the vibrations. We went into an escalator. Than into another corridor which had daylight.

Finally we entered into a brand new room filled with daylight which was 227.

I was there alone for a while that I thought I was forgotten. I waited on for someone to come in. I was nearly going to burst out crying as long as it was not something I was expecting. I felt so solitary in that intensive care unit that I thought I would enter into a room with lots of people clapping hands. There was nobody. I felt afraid for a second but than my father and mother came in. They thought I would come later but I arrived earlier than they expected. They were happy to see me. I was not allowed to have any visitors.

I later learned that my surgery took longer than they all expected. The tumor was bigger than they suspected. So the surgery became much more difficult that everyone that was waiting for me outside was terrified. When they found out that the surgery went well, they all cried together. I was alive. The tumor was clean as they thought it to be so I survived.

Our prayers were heard.

CHAPTER XIV

Last 7 Days in Room 227

As you could see there are two number twos and a seven in this title. Seven, which means miracles in life in numerology, has played a big role in that wonderful one week. That room was my miracle because lots of great people came in and out of it. Two means signs that come into our thoughts, sight or hearing. Every night when everyone felt asleep, I was awake in pain. I had too much to overview my life, question and elevate my self. I had long hours to pray, to listen and to learn to believe. I had signs every night in my thoughts. Than in the mornings when amazing, bright and shinning people such as nurses, attendants, assistants, cleaners and doctors visited my room, they thought me great lessons as miracles. They always showed me respect, tenderness, kindness and love. My room was a total bliss with its number and visitors.

My room attendant who was in charge to hold and straighten me up in my bed, helped me to walk me to the bathroom, washed my hair, helped me to take a shower and always told me cheerful stories and sang me songs. Her name was Ayşe. She felt my pain and she built an empathy with me. She was a short, chubby, happy lady with pink cheeks. She was so strong that she could have pulled me with one arm and put me in a wheel chair with one shift. She came every morning to check my bed sheets and change them in a second. I felt so lucky to have her to look after me. Also having clean sheets every morning after a long sweaty night was like a five star hotel treatment for me.

When I first saw Ayşe, she had no expression on her face but just tiredness. I saw the light in her eyes and even if I had difficulty to speak, I asked her name. She was very surprised with my interest and affection that I did not understood. She introduced herself and put a big warm smile on her face. The following days, she only smiled when she entered my room, asked my mood which was happy and grateful and shared her cheerful stories about her family. She was always very tender with me. She said she saw the light in my eyes that she even started to pray aloud every time she held me up. She sang me songs when she brushed my hair. I was the same age with her daughter that maybe she felt a deeper connection.

Today when I think of her, I can only smile.

When it was Ayşe's day off than there was Mustafa. He was a tall, thin and a strong man. He was in charge to change the sheets and check the needs of the room. I was so lucky that I was not sharing my room with any other patient but only my mother who stayed with me during that whole week. She was exceptional. My mother checked my urine every morning, calculated the liters of water I consumed, fed me like a small baby. She held my head every time I drank water. For other tasks that she could not handle there was Mustafa, who was a sad and harsh looking man. When I introduced myself to him, he changed his attitude as well.

Every morning he would first stop at my room to say hello. I never expected anything from them but gave love to them without asking back and in return they tenderly replied. I was so lucky to have those wonderful angels around me. They motivated me every morning and made me smile. I realized that whatever I do, whatever action or thought I choose, universe was replying back to me as a mirror. I smiled so they did. I felt bad and they did…

* * *

The most heart touching story that I shared with my mother was the first night in my room after my surgery. Night watch nurses were very professional. They were on attention all the moment of the night. The most difficult time of the day was the nights and a specially my first night.

I remember a moment that I wished for going back to the intensive care room. It was probably 8pm that they came into my room and checked my situation and gave my medicines. Than they checked my serum filled with morphine. It was dripping fine. My mother looked into my eyes and gave me a kiss. She talked to me for a while than made her bed and went in for a sleep. She asked me to wake her up when I needed. I said I was fine but I forgot that I was not able to shout out.

I was so drowsy that I fell a sleep. In the middle of the night, around 2 a.m., I woke up with a strong pain like the ones in the intensive care room. I wanted to scream out with pain but I could not. It was like trying to wake up from a nightmare but was not able to. I called out my mother slowly but she fell into a deep sleep that she could not hear my whispers for help. I did not know how to call on the nurses as well. After four or five attempts of calling out for help, my mother heard me and woke up. I told her to call the nurses but she was half awake that she did not understand me. She was just staring at me blank.

I found the rope to pull myself up from the bed to get out. It was my first night that it was like a magic for me to be able to pull myself up with that much pain. Maybe it was a God given strength at that time. I just wanted to stand up and went to the corridor to find the nurses. My mother was terrified when she saw that I pulled myself up. Well I was still strong after working out with Tony Hill for two months. Next, I pulled my legs out of the bed. My mother came back to her senses that she asked me what I was doing. I told her that I was going to run away. She was not aware of what she was doing that she started to laugh and was not able to stop. She had a nervous breakdown.

I became so mad that I started to hit the bed. Suddenly I bended to the side and got stuck with pain.

I was not able to move an inch. I started to cry out with tears running down my face and shout out with a small whisper 'HeLP!' Suddenly my mother stopped laughing and asked herself what she was doing. She had a terror in her eyes and also guilt. She got back to her senses one more time. She ran outside and came back with a nurse.

Nurse looked at me and was terrified. She said she was not allowed to give me any more painkillers because they were very strong and I was on the limit. My mother started to beg her because she knew that if I said I had pain I must have lots of pain. Also I was sweating like crazy. It was as if I was forgotten under the rain. It proved her how much pain I was in.

She came back with a night doctor and afterwards they brought in a bigger bottle of medicine. They changed the bottles of morphine with a higher dosage. They checked it several times and asked me to wait for a minute. I thought I was going to die that night but after the doctor showed up and changed the doze everything started to slow down. I was druged. I started to feel drowsy. My body started to get sleepy. Than I thought I was wetting my pants again. I hated the feeling but I had no other choice. I felt the whole sweat on my body that stuck me to the pillow. Actually my bed was damp with sweat. So my mother changed my t-shirt. I was not able to move any part of my body.

When I felt that dozy I thought to myself that I should have chose the pain instead of that unconscious mind. I felt a sleep with my mother's cries and apologies.

Breathing Therapies

My doctors checked me every morning. I felt lucky to have them available. They were checking my lungs, which was very important as long as the lungs were shut down during the surgery. I had to work on them to open my breathing. I was given exercises everyday. I was blowing balloons and also into a special machine which had three balls in it. I had to hit the three different colored balls to the head of the machine with one blow through a tube coming out of it from its side. It was such a difficult and painful task. I hated it.

I also had to walk the corridor three times a day, which was taking a minute for everyone but hours for me. It was a very long fifteen minutes walk for me. I was feeling every muscle and bone through each movement. I was breathing so slowly and hard that I was not able to speak when I was walking. Every step at a time was moving with awareness and care as I used to do in my meditations. Even eating my meals and taking medicines were like exercising for me that the days were going very fast for me. I had difficulty holding the silverware and carrying them to my mouth. I was very thankful for every each food I was able to swallow because it was extremely hard. I realized how important it was to do daily tasks. The things that were very basic and simple tasks to me before became very complicated to me. Even asking for help when I needed after so much effort was so difficult that sometimes I skipped and slept on it. Through patience and time I came over everything. Love and care motivated me. Prayer made me strong.

* * *

One day, I remember Mustafa so sad and worried for me. He was looking pale that I got worried for him as well. He said he felt gloomy because of my slow recovery. He said that I was supposed to do my exercises much easier than the other patients as long as I was younger than them. He witnessed my hard work and eagerness to process but was not able to see any difference. He wanted me to get well soon and leave the hospital. He knew that if I would need to stay longer than expected than I would start loosing my faith and motivation. He said he had witnessed it in other patients and experienced it in the past.

The doctors had given me the box with balls to open my lungs. I was blowing into that box four times a day. It was very difficult for me that I always tried to skip it but never had a chance with my mother's careful eyes staring onto me. The tool had three departments in it with three balls, white, red and blue. There was a tube coming from the side of the tool that I had to blow into it through that tube. When I was able to blow hard enough three of the balls would hit the top of the plastic box. However I was not even able to hit one ball to the ceiling. It was always going half way and than down. I was not able to breathe fully, eat properly and even talk aloud. Everyone told me that with practice, I would first hit one than two and lastly three of the balls together. That exercise would also help me to improve in other areas. It became my nightmare. I was not able to do it.

Every morning doctors were coming in and asking me to show them what I did but I was same. I felt like a student cheating in exams but I was not. They were making me feel guilty. Mustafa was also coming in every morning to check on how many balls I was able to hit even if it was not his duty. He just wanted me to heal fast. When he heard that there was no achievement, he became very worried because there were old people in my corridor that were able to do much better than me. He was very worried and went home.

Next morning he came in very cheerful. He asked me to try, saw that I could not than he took the tool from my hand and went outside. When he came back in five minutes, he was holding a brand new one in his hand. He opened the box and game me the tool and asked me to try again. So I did and I hit two balls at the first try. We were all very surprised and started to laugh. They were all laughing from happiness. I asked him how he knew that the tool was broken. He said he had a dream that the tool was broken. He must have thought about it so hard that he saw it in his dreams. Thank God that he was there for me. He was a miracle man.

* * *

I also had wonderful nurses. Every morning they came into my room to give me lots of medicines in different colors, gave me shots, checked my serums, cables and tubes, oxygen mask, fever, blood pressure and heart beats to give me more or less medicines. One early morning one of the nurses entered my room. It must have been Saturday that there was a cheerful songs playing outside, drums were beating for a wedding, than suddenly a mosque started to give the morning prayer out loud. I was filled with silence and peace. My nurse was there to give me shots. He looked at me and said something that I would never forget:

- Look at this life at the mosque there is a funeral because they are reading the funeral prayers, and at the sight they are playing drums probably for a wedding and here in the hospital a baby is probably born. Ones life taken and another's given in celebration that's how beautiful life is…

Than we were back into our silence as my blood filled in the tube that he took the needle away. I breathed in as he took it out. After, he walked away with my blood on his tray. I was tearful. I never thought of life as that. I was watching the same window every morning and night, the view was same but the story was different every day. All I needed was to have a different perspective.

* * *

We all had our share of laughter in that room. I remember my phone was ringing one day as a duck. The nurses got scared and I told them that the urine tray in the toilet, which is called 'duck', has just woken up. The nurses looked into each other and burst out laughing.

My father made jokes every day. I was asking him to stop that my scars would not hurt. However as soon as he stopped, I was starting to make jokes. We used laughter as our medicine. The time would not pass without them. I was seeing the other patients with less difficult matters with a strong sadness and worry in their eyes. I was shaking their hands and saying hello to them. All I wanted was to spread the good vibes to our corridor for healing.

It helped me.

Happy Birthday to me

Everyday was a different story. I was watching television in the room in order to fall asleep. I was watching the baby channels because I was not able to follow the motions on the tube. Actions were making me sick. Noises were giving me terrible headaches. I did not want to get excited than I would faint. It was amazing that every motion, emotion, and gesture was connected to my heart. I have always been against painkillers but here I was asking for them.

Every night nurses would come for the night watch. They will give medicines and check my situation and leave. It was a long process but always needed. I was making my toilet in a special tray that they asked me. They would calculate the amount of water that I drank and the urine that came out of my system. The body was a miracle itself. If one of the organs were not working properly, the urine that you did not even think of everyday would become your gold. They ask me every morning and night that I were constipated or not in order to evaluate my whole systems. I was able to feel every muscle in my body when I used the bathroom and thank God that my system was working fine. I never thought in my whole life that I would give a report to a nurse about my toilet habits but I did when I had to.

All the nurses gave me compliments about my positive attitude, laughter and jokes. I was filled with joy and I had to. If I would not feel the joy than I would live hell in the hospital like the lady staying in my opposite room. She had an easier operation than mine but she was so unhappy that nobody wanted to stop by her room.

One day when I was doing my daily exercise of walking. I came out of my room very slowly and walked to my next room, I visited that lady's room. She was a very old lady probably around her eighties. She was looking very sad and lonely with her nanny sitting next to her bed. As soon as I entered into her room through her welcoming open door after my knock, they turned their head to see their visitor. I introduced myself and explained my situation. Afterwards wished her to get well soon. They had a big surprise on their face and just nodded. The nanny thanked and went back to her complaining routine. The old lady was in surprise when she saw my visit. Maybe they found my action rude. Maybe she could not believe her eyes that a young girl was staying on her floor and had a heart surgery like her. Something might have touched her heart and might have brought some courage like I wanted. The next following days she stopped yelling.

When my walking started I met with all the other patients and their guests. I was unnoticeable with my pink pajamas and big white bunny slippers. They were calling me bunny girl. AS a bunny girl everyday ı was making a process and walking a bit faster than before. Everyday was a little progress. I was singing Rocky Balboa songs during my exercises to motivate myself. My mother was calling me The Tiger.

Well I was carrying a dragon inside me.

* * *

One afternoon my nurse came with a stroller into my room. He said he would clean my stitches and it was the first time I saw my scars. It was fairly small for a heart surgery. Thanks to technology and Da Vinci robot. I only had five stars where they made small holes for the robot to enter. Than there was a large scar underneath my right breast when they found out about the size of the tumor. They needed to cut to get in. My doctor did an esthetic stitching like the plastic surgeons do so that I would not have a terrible mark. However I was shocked when I first saw it. I chose to look another way and saw my fathers face. He was directly looking with a curious face and became whole white. He was probably thinking that his only little girl was hurt that he could not do anything to stop.

I breathed in hard that I did not feel any pain. Than I had the courage to ask what was the thing that I was feeling underneath my chest. The nurse told me that it was the drain and some other procedures that they put inside me. I felt like a metal hot pad was placed inside me. I was wondering how they would take that thing out.

Days passed and lots of guests came to visit me. They all brought me gifts. The room was getting more cozy and colorful everyday. My mother was so nervous that every day she was eating chocolate nonstop. She gained ten pounds in five days. She was getting filled like a balloon. She was running in and out of the room to check the nurses, control the flow of the guests because I was not allowed to have guests during my whole stay. They brought me balloons, chocolates, teddy bears, Mickey Mouse, t-shirts, heart shaped pillows, Turkish delights, shampoos, colognes, and many more gifts. I was only able to see them waving at me from the door. I was hardly waving back at them. I was not allowed to have visitors but their gifts became a placement of them.

The nights were all right. I learned to live with the pain day by day. When I woke up in the middle of the nights, I was watching the clouds and searching for signs. I was looking at the windows and the different shades of dark blue in the sky. My favorite time was 5 a.m., which was the early morning prayers. I would cry silently and pray God to save my life and my loving parents. I was blessed with this wealth. I asked God to forgive me for the times that I did not realize my wealth and had a pride to ask for more. I cried every morning to ask for forgiveness.

Than when the mornings came my beautiful nurses would wake me up with a cup filled with colorful medicines. I was thinking how stupid I was before to promise not to have a single medicine in my life. Whatever I said I would never do, I was always meant to do at the end. My grandmother always thought me not to talk big but careful. I thought I listened to her but I realized in the hospital that I did not. I apologized and forgave myself.

* * *

One afternoon a nurse entered into my room. He was a tall handsome man that I never seen before. He was very serious and looked very professional. He said he came from the intensive care room to take my drain out. He said it would be short and brief that he would not put me to sleep.

I said ok as long as I had no other choice. I was so happy that finally they would take it out as long as it stood longer than the doctors expected. He asked the assistant nurse to bring the stroller. It was the biggest stroller I have seen since my stay. He put down so many tools on the bed. He was putting them down in an order. He seemed like he had to be fast. He looked at me and said

"Well it might hurt a bit but not much so that I would ask you to take a deep breath and look away."

I said "OK"

I looked away and started to murmur a song. He started to count and pull a long string out of my chest. I moved up like a small fish with a small jump. I said

"It hurts but I am fine. Are we done?"

"Unfortunately not but this would be the last, so please sing another song."

So I started to sing… Happy Birthday to MeeEEEEEEE!!!

When it came towards the end it was sounding more like a heightened volume with pain. I was out of breath and said it hurt more so it must be the end.

He said "I am sorry. Unfortunately not please sign another birthday song, a third person is born today."

I was devastated. I did not believe my ears. I looked away and saw my mother looking away and holding her mouth closed. She was crumbled in her chair like a small child and looking pale. I did not know why she stayed there. Probably she knew and she wanted to be with me. So I looked away again and found my mothers eye and started to sign and when I came to the middle; I roared like a tiger. Maybe I roared like a bear that it no longer became a birthday song.

I saw the nurse's right arm extended from his left towards the right until its last reach. I saw a huge strain came out of me that I could not believe my eyes. When he threw it into his dispenser it even made a clicking sound. That day was my third birthday. A monster was born with a roar.

After that day, I promised my self that I would sign a birthday song cheerfully for myself every each birthday no matter what. I would be grateful for my life. I will be thankful for every moment.

My mother had tears in her eyes. When the nurse was done and started to gather his tool. I was drowsy with pain that I was hardly breathing. I never had a gun shot but my eyes burst out as in the movies after having a gun shot. I thanked God that I never had a gun shot.

During my seven days of stay probably a baby was born, a funeral was gone, a wedding was heard, and certainly three birthday songs were sang by me.

CHAPTER XV

Heading for Home

Ten days were gone so fast in Florence Nightingale Hospital. Finally the day came for me to leave and head to my parents' house. I was able to walk around slowly but carefully well that it was my time to check out. There was some anxiety and insecurity within me. The care in the hospital was perfect that I was worried not to find it at home. I was told that most of the patients feels the same before leaving the hospital. It made me feel safer.

There were questions and anxious thoughts swimming in my head just like the time before going to the hospital. It was like moving to a new house. I was so used to the routine of the hospital. Change was good but also scary. However it was time to move on and trust. I realized the fear inside me so I had to learn to accept it. Time would heal all as it did before. Anxiety was not the solution that I chose to trust the best outcome. Most difficult stage of the process was over. Doctors had done the last check ups and found me well to leave. I was told to keep myself motivated and not to loose the faith on myself.

I cried all the way to my house because I did not want to leave the nurses, attendants, room cleaners and housekeepers behind me. I wanted them all to come along with us. I loved their warmth, love and careful friendliness. As I was thinking of their faces and memories, I was not able to hold myself but only cry. I was like a small kid while I was looking for handkerchiefs at the back seat. Probably, I became too sensitive after the surgery. It became too easy for me to cry. I changed enormously. I became a quitter, sensitive and much more loving person.

I felt as if all my ices melted in that hospital room. I knew I would miss their warm happy faces. I had a long warm farewell with every each of them. They chose me to be the best patient of the month as a joke. We exchanged our blessings and prayers. I gave Ayse my lucky bracelet as a souvenir. She was very touched and wore it to bring her luck. I was picturing all the moments we had together in the hospital and cried for every each face of them and all the moments we we shared together all through the way home. I believe their care and friendly attitude has touched my heart very deeply. I was filled with bliss inside me. I felt them as a family during those ten days. The intense hope and faith that I carried in the hospital has made some kind of strong bond between them and me. I was hearing a melody in my ears kind of a farewell song that I could not stop.

Welcome

My ears were ringing because my grandparents were anxiously waiting for me at home. It was a superstitious belief in my culture that said if someone talks or thinks about you than your ears would start to ring. I was watching the road passing by me as the time was passing. I was daydreaming of my house and parents. We were driving in my father's car. My mother was sitting in the front and I was silently crying at the back seat. It was kind of dramatic. In order to smile, I dreamed of my house.

I was trying to guess the favorite meals that they might have cooked for me. I was dreaming of a huge welcome. However, I figured out that I did not have one as long as I was not allowed to have visitors. I only needed to rest. I did not even have the strength to come out of the car and walk home. As I entered into the house my dreams of gathering around the table disappeared. I realized I only needed to find a bed to lay and sleep. I had so much pain.

Family is the best gift life could offer to a person. We were born with a family but also some people that we met through our lives become occasional family to us. The people that I met in the hospital felt like one of those occasional families with their care, warmth, love and light. I was lucky that my family was always there for me. I am still lucky that my family is always here for me.

New Chapter of my Life

I was so lucky that I was able to leave the hospital and head to my house. I was so excited to see my family, friends, and also my two tiny dogs. But I was also sad to leave all the good people and memories behind me. A new chapter of my life was opening up for me at that moment. I was like a newborn baby that was able to talk and walk who was feeling the rhythm of life with a new engine. The engine did not come up with an operating manual but with care and love we both would adapt to each other. An adaptation time has started with pain when I woke up in the intensive care room. Through time it became lesser and thought me to be patient. Every beginning was beautiful but also difficult. The thing that was keeping me strong was having persuasion for better life no matter what was going on around me. I learned to watch every instance with faith and taking it as a life lesson. Nothing was my enemy even if it hurt. Everything was for my goodness as long it came from God. This faith came to me after my harsh experience in that hospital. I learned to believe in God in a stronger way because I realized after every each of my each prayer I had an answer.

First following days were so difficult as I imagined. It was difficult to adapt to my surrounding. Every night was sleepless with so much pain. I did not have the strong medicines or painkillers that I had in the hospital. There was not any one to ask for at home when I had felt the pain. Days were going fast and smooth but not easy. I was trying to rest during the day because I knew that pain would always hit me at nights. I was hardly breathing, and moving in bed that it was not very usual. I was having high temperatures and dizziness all the time. I wished to toss and turn t nights but I had no chance to do it. I always had the heaviness on one side and numbness on my whole body that was not allowing me.

My mother would put me to bed as a small child every night. She would position my pillows and bed than leave a glass of water beside me. She laid me to bed with one position and I would stay in that way since I call her for help. Therefor I was calling her many times at night that she was not able to have a good sleep. My legs and arms were sleepy that I was hardly walking but I needed to have toilet visits frequently at night that I needed assistance. They were all very embarrassing for me. The reason was that I was not a person that could ask for help easily even if it was my mother. I had difficulty calling on people in need. It made me furious at nights that my pain was growing harsher. When the morning came, I was waking up with my mothers call for breakfast. I had to wake up early and have an early breakfast so that I would not skip any medicine. It was very annoying as well as long as I had less pain in the mornings and wanted to sleep. My mother did not have a different choice.

Medicines were making me drowsy all through the day, which was very uncomfortable. It was a nightmare to take a shower. I was sitting on a chair in the bathtub and wait on my mother to wash me. She was putting plastic ducks in the bathtub to make me laugh. We were singing songs to make the experience a bit easier for me. It felt like I was back to childhood. We were talking about my childhood and how my mother was taking care of me when I was a small baby. It was so strange that I felt as if I was reborn.

My long hair was taking hours to get washed and dried that it was making me breathless. I was only wishing to have a haircut. It took me two years to grow my hair that long but that pain could not stop me wishing for a haircut. My only wish was to get a haircut when they allowed me to get out of the house. I even asked my mother to cut them for me but she did not dare to do. Every little movement was like heavy lifting for me. Through time it became a bit easier but still it was not looking normal to my parents. We were doubtful about my recovery.

I was not allowed to have visitors in the house as long as my immune system was still low. It was winter that everyone was catching a cold that they were a danger for me. Some of my best friends came for a very short visit. It was so difficult to sit with them and talk but I never resisted them and did my best. I did not want anybody to feel bad for me. I was only thankful to them for their visits. I needed to stand or sit strong and tall that I would believe I was getting well.

Slow Recovery

Finally we accepted that my condition was not getting better but going for worse. I was supposed to be good after two weeks but was getting sicker. I became paler and more tired. We decided to see the doctors again. We called them several times and had the chance to get an appointment. It was very difficult for me to go back to that hospital. I was afraid to enter through those doors again. It was scary to leave it two weeks before and than it became difficult to go back there. I did not know what kind of trauma I was in.

In the hospital my mother was running around as usual. She was trying to find the doctors and get things done quicker. She had a very strong empathy with me that she was acting as if she was feeling my pain. She was like my other half. She would smile when I did and frown when I was sad. I realized how dear my mother was to me through those days. She ran around and arranged the appointments at the same place so that I would not need to walk around much. They did some scans, blood tests and checkups. They analyzed them and they figured out that I was going through a very rare symptom that some patients had after surgeries. I was kind of tired of having rare symptoms. The doctor explained it to us.

'After some of the difficult heart surgeries, the heart would react by its outer layer getting swollen, which was causing extra ordinary pain in the chest of the patient. Some kind of liquid would form which would cause the outer layer to react by getting thicker. In the past, taking a second surgery could only heal the problem. The liquid formed on the outer layer of the heart would be drawn with a special injector. However, thanks to technology and the doctor who has found a special medicine with his name on it. He cured this problem by only taking pills. It would have some side effects such as numbness and drowsiness but some extra medicines that I would prescribe would balance it.'

So he did write me a long list of medicines. I was happy that I got away this problem by only taking medicines. I did not question why I was in that small percentage of patients to experience this problem but only tried to stay positive. I was only hoping for taking many different medicines would not cause me other problems. But unfortunately they did. I was having diarrhea, numbness, drowsiness, sleepiness, high temperatures, high blood pressures, extra chest pains and my whole body was getting extra swollen after taking those pills. I started to be nervous and fed up with all the pain I was experiencing. My only medicine was my patience but I was out of it.

I was only wishing for a healing miracle.

My shaman pets

Every night, my older dog chose to sit on my numb leg for one hour. She would come next to me and would push away my hands to open a space on my lap than she would sit quietly without moving. She eased my pain with her warmth and good energy. When she stood up, she was feeling drowsy and tired and chose to sleep for long hours. It was an amazing process. She was choosing to heal me with her own will. My other younger dog would also lie down under my armpit and put his head on my heart. He was a very hyper dog but when he came next to me he would just lay near me quietly. He would not move or step onto my body. He knew that I had pain.

The doctors told me that the numbness of my right leg was because of them cutting a small place to get in. Approximately it would take six months for the numbness to pass. There was no medicine or exercise that would help to shorten the time period. However my dogs shortened the time period to three months instead of six months that I was able to walk more stable. Both of my dogs were always there for me. I was so lucky to have a wonderful family beside me. They were my two tiny shamans. I felt even more connected to them after this surgery.

It took one month to heal the layer of the heart. My pain started to get lesser and easier through the days that I started to feel less nervous. I was not allowed to have any guests visiting my house for one month because of my low immune system. When they started to come with gifts and warm conversations time started to pass quicker and easier for me. I understood who was a real friend and who was not during that time. I never complained to anyone but just let the time show me my true friends. I accepted their apologies but most importantly tried to forgive them within me. I changed my life style, thoughts and belief system. Nothing became so important to me after the surgery but only my life.

Healing Gratitude

I thanked God that I experienced this illness because it helped me to realize how valuable is my health. It also thought me to eat healthier. I was only wishing to get well soon that I would be able to exercise and do some sports. I was very curious how my sleeping habits would be like after I got well. I knew that I was able to sleep well and easy in the past so I was not sure how a good sleep would felt like. I was very tired of having nightmares and waking up in the middle of sweaty nights.

I was dreaming of exercising, being healthy and happy. I was dreaming of running miles and miles without being breathless. I never had the chance to run for hours since my childhood. However, I was very thankful that through that process of getting born with uncomforting feeling, I understood how valuable and comfortable it was to be healthy. I was only praying God by thanking Him that he showed me how lucky I was lucky to be healthy.

I was thankful that I had the chance to learn and see how lucky I was. Through gratitude I stayed positive and saw the goodness in my slow recovery. It was a chance given to me to discover and understand myself. It was a call for me to realize how dear I was to life. I understood that there was a reason for me to be alive. I thought I might touch some people's life through my story or life that God has let me live.

I was only thankful…

Time was flying by and months were going fast. As the pain was going away I was feeling much freer. December went by with understanding the reason of the pain, and than Christmas came, followed by the new years.

The New Years Resolutions

Every New Year I was worried to find a nice dress to wear for the night and a nice bag that would go well with it. I was worried to find a party to attend or having a dinner reservation with my friends. I waited on my ex-boyfriend to call me the last two years for new years. He did call me in the first year right after we met but on the second new years we were separated and away. I was worried to get back with him. I only thought of him that I did not have fun. I did not understand how lucky I was to be able to live and be around.

At this year I thought about all the past new years and wasted times. I realized I lost the meaning of happiness, as I grew older. I only partied without thinking or finding the meaning behind the relations. I was only there in the crowd but I was lost in an empty space. I had so many people around me but few valuable ones. I was drinking, smoking, laughing hard without conscious and was numb in my heart. So I decided to think different this year that I thought to write down my findings. I made new years resolutions as to have healthier life style and relationships. So this new years began different and I knew that it would continue to be different. As I changed the way of my thinking, the life ahead of me was changing by reflecting my choices.

This year would be different. I was only able to stay at home. I was only able to fit into one dress. I was not allowed to drink. I was not capable of staying late. It sounded depressing but it was the best new years night ever for me. All I had was love and family.

Pure White Snow

It was snowing mad outside that our garden was all in white. We decorated the Christmas tree a month before that it was ready for the New Years eve. My mother made a nice menu and she invited my grandparents. Everybody was excited in the house. My mother was anxiously cooking to get the list ready. It took her the whole day to cook them. I was able to stand by her and watch her. I helped her to chop some vegetables slowly and carefully. We were making jokes, singing and laughing by the oven. It was a cozy family day for us. Than the night came that we prepared ourselves for the night.

My grandparents came to our house on time. They were also dressed up and smelling nice. We all gathered in the living room and started to have warm conversations. I was feeling tired all the time that they were the ones making conversations. I was only happy to watch them. It was a gift to be at home and able to celebrate a new year. I was thinking to myself that snake year would be coming soon and it would be the year of health and healing. I was only wishing for my whole family to gather around many more dinner tables. We enjoyed all the beautiful courses that my mother prepared for us. Than we had our desert that my grandmother made which was delicious as well. We were all delighted to be together. My grandparents kept thanking that I was able to be with them. We made conversations.

At that night, I decided to write this book.

CHAPTER XVI

My new apartment and neighborhood

After new years, I moved back to my own apartment with my mother. I was so surprised when I entered into the house. I have not been there since we signed the rental contracts and my mother made a surprise for me. She renovated the flat. All the walls were painted. The bathrooms and the kitchen tiles were changed. It was a whole new place. It was brighter and much more nicer than the time we rented it. I was so happy to be there. My bedroom was big and spacious with a balcony filled with my flowers, plants and pots. I had new curtains in pink and my walls were in color of light green. It was very peaceful and cozy. My mother wanted me to be renewed and happy when I got back to my new house. We tossed for new year, new house, new energies and a brand new heart that would bring all the best possible outcomes.

My mother was so sad and moved with my past surgery that she was doing all the best possible things for me without asking me. She wanted to surprise me and made me happy that she would also feel free. We were all very touched by the process that I went through so we were traumatized. As a family we were filled with gratitude that everything went well at the end but still we were all still in shock. I knew that there were many more young patients, children and even babies that went through terrible surgeries and needed to live in the worst conditions but still I was in shock for what I went through. It took me a very long time to get back to my self. I became traumatized and a bit depressed. I was worried about my condition but was also aware that everything was going for the better. I was questioning why and how for the situation but than thanking for the results. I thought that moving to my new apartment would change my mood and motivate me.

I was so happy to be back in my old neighborhood. It was lively and crowded in the area that I live. There is a restaurant right across my house called Mahalle, which means neighborhood, and it is the cornerstone of my street. Everybody that lived around always meets there for lunch or dinner. They have very god live music on the weekends that I hear people's conversations and laugh. The place cheers up the area and always lightens up my mood. I know its owners whom became my very close friends after my surgery. The owners are as friendly and lively as their restaurant. Their welcoming and loving attitude gives energy to their place that it feels like a cozy home. The owner's sister is going through cancer that they know the importance of health. Therefor they easily gave empathy and comfort to my family's situation and me. We shared very friendly conversations in a very short time and became really good friends.

I started to walk to the restaurant every morning and get my morning herbal teas to talk with my friends. I also made new friends. They always greeted me with enthusiasm and kept motivated me. I was aware that my circle of friends was changing for better. I looked forward to my mornings to have my omelets and have lovely conversations with the bar tender called Fatos. She and I started know each other very well through time that we both enjoyed our conversations. We were watching the street, making comments about the weather or politics, talking on daily news and my lovely dog. There are people walking by, cats and dogs barking at each other, lots of cars passing and mostly stuck in the street that it is not silent like my parents house on Ihlamur Street (Linden Street). There is always something to watch and talk about that I became like elder people. However as I imagined it started to give some joy to me. I guess I needed some rest and learn to enjoy free time. I started to feel as if I was healing faster.

Everybody was asking for me. They were all so worried for me. The pharmacist, Mahalle, the supermarket, the public parking attendants, the hairdressers, bakers, butchers, grocery store, antique shop, and souvenir shop's owners, and also my neighbors were all waiting for my arrival. They greeted me and sent their good wishes. I was so happy to be remembered and thought. It sometimes felt strange to be back but always good that I was little by little getting back to my old routine. It felt like a long time. I felt so lucky to be back and be in a brand new place. I knew that it would bring me a change. The new apartment's number was 5 and it was my lucky number so what more could I ask.

Living Conditions

I still needed some care and assistance. I was having difficulty with long distance walks and was not able to take care of my own needs easily. My mother was there for me since the beginning. She understood my needs and eagerness to go back to my own life routine so that she accepted my offer to move in with me since I get better. She helped me to walk the dogs, cook my meals and also have my daily exercises. This period of time was a blessing for me. My relationship with my parents became more valuable and intense. We all realized how difficult we were to each other in the past so that we gave up on the control issues we had with each other and accepted each other with mutual understanding.

When I got back to my apartment, I decided to use the entire alternative healing methods that I could find in order to ease my pain faster. I knew that I was having some difficult time physically, emotionally and also psychologically that I had to try every method in order to move forward. The trauma of the surgery was following me every time I looked at the mirror. I was seeing nightmares every night I slept and was hardly having patience for the pain. I felt that I was afraid that I could have all the experiences again or would never be able to heal even if I was getting better. I had to find a way to give me more patience and understanding. I needed a detox for my body and soul.

I decided to see my breathing therapist. I made an appointment with her and decided to visit her studio, which was two blocks away from me and would normally take five minutes to walk.

Alternative Treatments

I have decided to make the time go easier for me. All I wanted was to heal fast and went back to my usual routine. I was not able to work. My next solo exhibition was canceled. I was disappointed with it but also encouraging myself that one day I would be fine to stand up and continue on my work. I was praying every each day that I would be able to paint again. I had finished the half of the new series before the surgery but I did not have the strength to stand up for making the other half. I was not even able to stand up for an hour or just sit to paint. I was only able to take small walks outside. I was feeling lucky if I was able to walk the dog once a day. I realized that I had difficulty with my breathing whenever my heart rate rose so my first choice was to see my breathing therapist that I met a year before my surgery. I believed it would help to increase my motivation.

Breathing Therapy:

A year before my surgery I met my breathing therapist, Duygu Keçecioğlu, through email. Her breathing studio's newsletter dropped into my mailbox by mistake. She does not know how her email reached me and I don't know how she found me. The newsletters were only for her clients. It was a great coincidence.

All I wanted was to find a breathing therapist at that time and one day I received her email filled with introduction of her therapies. We were meant to meet. I took a group of my friends to visit her studio at that time. She asked me how I found her and I told her that she had found me. We were both surprised and were happy that email reached to the wrong address but found its place. So I took one of her breathing sessions to learn the techniques and apply to my meditations. I practiced it as she told me for couple of months and later lost myself in my work that forgotten it.

A year after my first meeting with Duygu, I went to see her with my mother. I had difficulty going to places by walk that my mother joined me. We both had a session together and my mother decided that she needed to take more sessions with her. She realized that she was filled with stress and fear as I was after what we had gone through. We started to visit Duygu's office separately once a week for one month. Through time I was healing for better that I was able to walk to her place alone. Her office was two blocks away from me, which was taking five minutes of walk a year before to get to her place, but at that time it was taking me twenty minutes. Her therapies opened up my breathing that time started to shorten up. It was motivating me and helping me to clear my fear and raising my energy level.

During her breathing therapy, she was using chakra therapy oils and Tibetan bowls after repeating her positive affirmations. She would control my breathing flow through her hands and repeat positive affirmations depending on my blocked chakra areas. I would start to feel numb on the areas that she was opening up. I remember myself coughing for long minutes when she was working on my throat. She was a great gift during my convalescence. There were thirty minutes therapy sessions before the breathing work. Duygu helped me to overcome my traumas of the surgery. My biggest fear at that time was starting to take steroids because of my anti-medicine attitude. She helped me to change my attitude towards medicines during her talking sessions. She asked me to see all my medicines as a part of my healing process and learn to love them and thank them. I realized that I needed to have gratitude towards them and send gratitude to every each of them. I started to make a small prayer for my medicines before taking them so that they would heal me for better. It helped a lot. I started to have faster results.

After I returned back to my house, which was almost four months after my surgery, the problem with the outer layer of my heart was not cured. So I was having difficulty with sleeping, walking, and even breathing. My cardiologist was very patient with me but he could not figure out the problem. He was also worried that valve of my heart was making leakage. At one point he told me that he was afraid that I would not be able to have my old condition back with the valve problem. I might even need to have another surgery in a coming up year. Another option would be starting taking steroids but he was not sure about the results. He has tried many different kinds of medicines other than steroids on me but they were not giving me better results. I was feeling weak, tired, breathless and sometimes drowsy. I was afraid that I would stay that way and live all my life with those medicines and never be able to paint as I used to. I realized how valuable my body and life was and how grateful I had to be with it. I was worried but also thankful that I was alive.

Domancic Bio-energy Therapy:

During that rough time breathing therapies helped me to ease the pain, stress level, concerns and the difficulty of breathing that came with it. Surprisingly, some breathing techniques that Duygu applied me helped to detox anesthetize out of my system faster than usual. However, I was still feeling tired during the days and hardly doing my daily activities. One day, Duygu told me that she knew a group of healers who were practicing Domancic Bio-Energy Therapy that she would like to introduce them to me.

I only needed to attend their sessions for four days for fifteen minutes or longer as I wished. I did not need to believe in them or do something for eztra. She said t many people were having miraculous results. I thought I would not loose anything. It was also for free. I thought I would also have a chance to meet wonderful new people. Therefor Duygu and I walked to the place where they were giving the sessions.

We arrived to the yoga center that they were giving sessions as visitors. We went into to the back room where they were doing the workshop. There were group of people sitting around in a circle in the living room. In the middle of the circle, the bio-energy healers were applying healing energy to the randomly picked visitors. I arrived there with difficulty and was not able to observe my surrounding well. I just found a chair and sat down to calm my beating heart. Duygu explained my situation quickly to her healer friends and asked them to take me right away. It was very obvious that I was hardly speaking or breathing because of the long walk that we took. As soon as I entered into the next room, they took a look at me and asked where I had the pain. I showed them my heart and explained the condition of the pain. They looked at me smiling with a small pity in their eyes. They told me that I was looking very pale so that they would take me to the middle of the circle right away.

They did not want me to wait after they heard about my problem. Four people circled me and put their warm hands on my heart. They started to move their hands in strange actions as if they were swiping away the dust of my body. Couple of minutes after their gestures, I was started to yawn and feel extremely sleepy. It was strange as long as I was sleepless and very awake for a very long time. I felt as if a heavy lift was coming off my body. I did not know how I would walk back to my house as long as I was feeling extremely sleepy. All I needed was to sleep for hours for a very long time but I was not able to with the pain. At that moment after the bio energy session, I felt a curtain of sleep dropped on my eyes. When I returned home I was having twelve hours of deep sleep. I was not able to fall a sleep before but after their each sessions I was feeling more and more sleepy. I slept nonstop for very long hours during the days and nights during that four days.

Four days have passed and I felt like I had less pain. I thought I was daydreaming at the beginning but it felt so real. I did not know how to approve it but I felt a change in my heart. I had an appointment with my cardiologist in that week after the four days of bio energy session. My cardiologist did his routine check with his eco machines to calculate the heart beatings and visualize the leakages in the valves. It took him a very long time to check this time because he looked very surprised and found some strange results. He said that he checked the condition of my heart and found out that the valve was healed in an unknown way. He was very surprised that the leakage disappeared in a week without doing some kind of different treatment. He was shocked. He could not understand how it could change in a week as long as he was trying to come to this result for the past three months. He asked me what I did different but I could not tell him anything. I knew that he would not believe me. Doctors generally had an attitude towards alternative treatments so I kept my silence. I did not want to face a disapproval again.

The only problem that was left was to heal the condition of the outer layer of my heart, which was swollen by carrying some liquid and causing me some extra pain. My cardiologist has directed me to see another doctor whom was the head of the cardiologist department in Florence Nightingale Hospital that I stayed during my surgery. My doctor wrote a long letter explaining my situation and gave me the blood test results and others to show the doctor.

Second Opinion

I took an appointment with the hospitals cardiologist within that week. I went to the hospital with my mother and waited there for long hours to be called and finally my time had come. We went to the counter and signed some papers and filled out some forms. Young assistant came and lead us to the doctors office. He was too busy that many people were waiting outside to be called. The assistant was waiting outside with a list of patients in her hand and running around to lead everyone. We waited long but thought to be lucky to be called.

We went into a dark office, which was probably changed from a patient room to a doctor's office. The doctor was a calm, tall and kind middle-aged man. He was listening to classical music in his small office. He was seeing patients in between his surgeries. Outside his office was a corridor of surgery rooms, which were busy with nurses and medical supplies and other doctors. He closed the doors to give his full attention to my mother and me.

I explained him my situation. He said he was so sorry to hear what I have been through at my young age and he found all the circumstances usual. He said that only other treatment would be taking steroids but he would not find them helpful. He said that I would need to take life easier now and then with less activities meaning less sports and painting. He asked me to take a quarter pain killer whenever I had the pains. I was shocked and hold myself not to cry there. I thought life would be easier for me after the surgery but it sounded to be more difficult and complicated. I knew that I was very lucky to be alive and in a good condition but I was hoping to be like my friends. I was expecting to be healed but unfortunately it sounded as I was already healed. However, I was imagining myself running, painting for hours with no difficulty and going out with friends as I used to.

I told him that I was not feeling well but he said it would be better. He asked me to be patient and taking things easier. He did not want to give me steroids and try the other treatment. He said that he found me at my best condition. All the pain was normal and I had to learn to live with it. I understood that there was not more to talk to him. I was only holding myself not to cry there which was putting me into more stress. So we thanked him and left his room. I was devastated.

I did not want to seem demoralized because my mother needed my support as well. She was looking pale and miserable but forcing herself to look strong. I said everything would be fine. I said to myself that 'I am lucky that I am alive'. This is a great life lesson given to me.

God is here to help us. I started to pray silently to calm myself down. I was praying and asking God for a miracle. I was just walking in the corridors of the hospital silently by praying.

Answered Prayer

At that instant, a hand touched my shoulder. I stopped walking and turned my head slowly and saw my heart surgeon. He had a big smile on his face and as soon as he looked into my eyes he looked worried. He told me that he was walking fast to get to his surgery on time and saw me walking alone in the corridor before entering his surgery. He realized that I was looking pale, walking too slow with a bad posture that he decided to stop.

He felt the urge to stop even if he was running late. I hardly smiled but was pleased to see him that I gave him my greetings. My mother showed up at that instant and helped me to talk to him. My doctor told us that I was not looking well because I was not standing straight. He said I must have had so much pain in order to have a posture like mine. He asked me to take an appointment with him urgently within that week. Than he looked straight into my eyes and promised me that he would put me back into my best condition even better than before. I was shocked because that was what I was praying for just a minute ago.

My mother was also very surprised because she had called my surgeon many times before but never received an answer. We never heard back from him after he prescribed me with some medicines for my heart valve and outer layer. It was very difficult to reach him. Everyone was hardly making an appointment with him. He was operating four people a day. He was a very well known doctor who has lived and worked in United States for years. He was known to introduce the robotic surgery to Turkey. So many people around Turkey and also neighboring countries were visiting the hospital and this doctor to have a surgery with the latest technology. It was a miracle that he was asking himself for us to make an appointment with him.

Right after hearing the words from the doctor we had the light in our eyes. My mother told me to wait in the corridor for her. She hurried to my surgeon's department on the other side of the hospital with a very quick pace that I would not be able to keep up. She ran to find the surgeon's assistant to get an appointment before it was too late. In one hour we were able to get an appointment with him. We waited in the waiting room anxiously seeing other people waiting. Some were foreigners talking in Arabic or other kinds of languages that I could not differentiate. It seemed as a different world to me. I was hearing my own heart rate from hunger and weakness after walking so much. We were so happy but also worried. However within my heart, I knew that my prayers were heard and whatever was next would only be for my highest good.

Couple of days later, we went back to the hospital for my appointment with my surgeon Dr. Berlhan Akpinar. He was very happy to see us. He was looking tired as long as it was his end of the day after his long heart operations.

He had big eyes with light inside. He was different from all the other doctors with his kind caring attitude. The light inside his eyes showed his love for his life purpose. Dr. Akpinar cared for his patients and had empathy for them. He examined me and asked us to get some scans, screenings and tests. Couple of hours later we were back in his office and found him at his desk examining the results. He was looking serious but also not worried. He started to explain us the results.

'The thickening of her heart's outer layer is still there. It is not as serious as before that she is not feeling severe pain as she used to. However this much of liquid in the layer of the heart causes her feel tired and gloomy. Unfortunately her time of healing took longer than we expected. The good news is that we still have cures to finish this last situation. You would not need to live with this pain but feel much better than before. So I will need to prescribe you Sezin, some steroid shots and also pills that you would need to take for two months.'

My mother asked if steroids would cause some problems. The doctor said none as long as I would be taking for a short period of time. I would only need to be careful when cutting them down because it would also take same amount of time. Steroids would help to heal the circumstances so that I would be able to feel stronger and more energetic. If I like I could choose to continue on eating healthy and cut down on salt and sugar.

He asked me to see him after two months. Afterwards I would pay him one more visit in order to see the final results after cutting down on the dozes of steroids. It would be my final four months of taking medicine. I was so happy that I would be cured. It was such a miraculous day for me to hear that I would be able to work better than before. I had a problem with taking medicine before but I thought of my breathing therapists advice. I learned to love steroids instead of hating them.

My medicines were an answered prayer so there was no reason to hate them but love them. I was so lucky that I was able to find the right treatment for me and also had the capability to get my medicines. I said to myself that I would learn to eat healthy and learn to love and respect my body as well. I knew that steroids were holding on to the water in the body and would make me swollen in the future so that I cut sugar and salt in my meals. I drank more water in order to detoxify and control the water level in my body. I respected to live with steroids so did them.

Through those four months I was able to feel the healing. I prayed God and angels. I continued with my breathing therapies. I went to see the best acupuncture doctor in Istanbul Dr. Erol Erguler whom was practicing many different kinds of alternative treatments. He became my new spiritual guidance.

Acupuncture Treatments

I heard about Dr. Erol Ergüler through a friend that came to visit me during my recovery stage. I heard that he was a very well known doctor that was practicing many different kinds of alternative treatments and helped my friend in her difficult times. So I took an appointment and found out that his office was walking distance to my house again. It only took me fifteen minutes of walking to get to his given address.

I walked into a very welcoming traditional office that was filled with Chinese symbols, crystals, Buddha statues and Eastern treatment books. Doctor was very calm and serene looking middle-aged man who had a soft smile on his face. He was very tranquil and relaxing so does his office with a small Chinese fountain placed at his entrance door. He introduced himself and asked me my reason for a visit. I explained him my surgery and what kinds of problems I was going through in that time. He listened to me carefully and quietly. Than he told me that I was in a recovery stage not only body wise but also mentally. Heart surgeries generally had after affects psychologically to patients that sometimes their behaviors changed. He had given a very beautiful example in order for me to understand.

'You had given your heart in the hands of surgeons for healing but they had put in knives and needles in to it. They have not finished by only that but also given you many medicines on top of it. You have told me that you were against medicine and have not taken any medicine before but chose to use organic methods. You also have not had any surgery before that this experience was totally new to you. So it is very usual for you to see nightmares and have sleepless nights. After the heart surgery you will experience a total bliss. There will be a raise in your comfort level that you have never experienced before in your life. For almost thirty years you have lived with a tumor in your heart that was holding you away from experiencing life in its fullest potential. Now that it is removed your blood circulation will raise, your oxygen level will be higher, your blood quality will be better so that you will experience a much more healthier life. You are always told with these kinds of information that makes you believe that you are lucky which is true but also not. The reason is that you went through so much pain and scary experiences through this time of healing. So it is very ordinary for you to be traumatized.'

He understood me in a small conversation I had given him. He said that I was going through a big trauma and under a fear of getting hurt again. Through my conversation he has realized that I was a very responsible and family oriented person that I had put myself in a pressure of taking care of my family's emotional problems through my illness. Therefore he advised me to experience his three different kinds of methods in order to clear this trauma and relax my mind and body in the coming future. Before starting these treatments, he wanted to practice a small test on me to understand the level of my concentration.

He had given me a stick with a glass ball tied at its end and asked me to hold it in one hand and let the ball hang down loose from the edge of his desk. As soon as I saw that tool, I remembered myself reading about it in one of Deepak Chopra's books. I recalled that it was used in meditations and also for healing panic attacks and ADD patients. When I told my knowledge about the tool to my doctor, he had a warm smile on his face and approved my realization. So he asked me to concentrate on the ball without moving my hand and only thinking of moving the ball to the sides so I did and the ball started to move. He asked me to think of the opposite so did the ball moved to the opposite directions. At last he asked me to think of stopping the ball and the ball slowly stopped where it started. I smiled at him and he told me that I successfully passed his test. He found me very well trained in meditation and my mind was in total focus and harmony.

I was surprised that years have really thought me a lot. Also it was very excited to be able to meet this interesting tool in the doctor's office. I read about it many years before and finally it was time to be introduced to it. Unfortunately, I would never guess to be introduced to it by some Turkish doctor as long as Turkish doctors were generally very traditional and against alternative treatments. However, Dr Ergüler was different. He could have been a traditional thyroid doctor but he has chosen to widen his wisdom in alternative treatments many years ago. He was one of the first doctors who had introduced different methods to Turkey. As he was talking about his background, he added that this kind of wisdom has given him the peace he has been looking for many years.

He used to be very against traditional alternative treatments and was even laughing at them. As years passed it started to gain his curiosity that he found himself studying them. He was able to enjoy his occupation more and more through his professional years in alternative treatment. He had a very wide knowledge in Eastern traditions and his awareness was very wide open. So that he was happily sharing his wisdom with his patients. When he saw my interest in these methods, he spoke more about them. I told him about my crystal collection and explained my use of them for healing. He reminded me to see them only as a tool between the higher self and me. A tool was only helping me to understand my ability to help myself. Then he went back to his quick test with the stick and the ball.

'All I wanted was to help you see the power of thought and way of thinking. Human body is very powerful that whatever we think and concentrate on can influence the way we live a qualified life. We are actually giving very strong signals to our every little sequence of our body by using our mind. When we are able to have focus and control on the way we think all the thought patterns would be able to slow down and be in peace. When we are able to achieve this kind of control then all we need to do is concentrate on what we are thinking. When we can think only the positive situations than our heart rate would slow down and give out more positive energies. After this kind of wisdom, we would be able to live a happier and much more healthier life. Now that we are introduced to the power of thinking and energy waves we are expending around, lets meet my machine here that can calculate them. Here is my machine that helps you to see the frequencies of your energy level by thinking positive or negative thoughts. Hold these metals that are connected to my machine please. Now think of your happiest moment in your life. Than we will see the frequencies getting higher than 0 pointed here. After you think of something negative, you will see them falling below 0'

So as the doctor said I thought of one of my happiest moments in my life. It was one of the surprise birthday party thrown to me by my mother. I remembered the time that I opened the door and saw all my wonderful friends staring at me. At that instant I heard a long strong beeping sound. Dr. Ergüler started to laugh and said you must have been very happy at that day. See that your frequency level just hit to the highest point. Than he asked me to think of my worst day ever which was the time that I heard my grandfather had a stroke. Than the machine started to give a slow ending noise. My doctor was as surprised as I was as long as I was able to change my mood very quickly only with a small memory. So he warned me again to think of only positive memories. He strongly advised me to stay at the present moment by holding good intentions. The experience I had at his office that day was a wonderful lesson to me.

Then he brought a tray of small oil bottles, which were named under the founder, as Bach Flower Therapy. He introduced me to the founder by telling me the history and the doctor's studies. All the bottles were filled with different kinds of flower oils that were healing different kinds of psychological issues. Those oils or some foods, spices or drinks all had some kind of energy that had an effect to higher or lower energy frequencies. For example as the doctor placed a cigarette on the machine's compartment, my frequency level was going down. Dr. Ergüler picked every each oil bottle and started to place them in the machine's compartment. He calculated my frequency level whichever bottles made my energy high, he separated them to the side. The chosen bottles would be the potential healer flower oil. Only taking a drop of that flower oil and mixing its small amount with water became my medicine for the following one month. After my bottle was ready, we have figured out that three different kinds of flowers were treating my three different kinds symptoms of my strong concerns at that time. One flower was for people who had gone through big traumas such as accidents or surgeries. The other flower was for people who were really tied to their family and strongly concerned about their health. The last flower was for people who were workaholics and concerned for their lack of time to work. So my list of flowers did really summarized my situation at that time.

I sprayed my small water bottles at my mouth three times a day. I was told to wake up early to get one spray of the water in the morning by holding only good intentions. Second time was in the afternoons after a long day and the last third spray was before going to bed early at nights. I did this for one month and a week later my mood started to change. My heart rate started to slow down. As my doctor said I visited him back two weeks later. This time he made me hypnosis. At the end of the hypnosis I visualized a symbol. I held the memory of that vision and practiced on it five times a day in my meditations. Through time the vision started to transform into different kinds of symbols. I was also told to work on those visions every time I was under stress or worry. So I did and through time I started to feel more relaxed and comfortable. I felt more peaceful and less in pain.

A month later I visited my doctor again for acupuncture. Forty-one needles were placed on my back. I was not feeling any one of the needles when placed on unproblematic areas on my back. But when placed on the blocked areas such as my heart chakra area on my back, I felt a strong pain sticking at my back. The room was very comfortable with the music choice I made. Doctor also placed a special heated pillow under my stomach filled with herbal leaves made in China. Special magnetic laser waves were given to the bed I laid in order to heal my blocked areas. I was so relaxed that I felt asleep with all those needles on my back. When the doctor came back to the room, he woke me up in order to take the needles. I was eased with a different kind of pain where the needles were after they were removed. Through days the pain disappeared and was placed with ease.

Dr Erol Ergüler became a great spiritual teacher to me. On the following days, I visited his office with different kinds of concerns. He was giving a treatment followed by a speech, which would open a different kind of awareness. He changed the way of my thinking and helped me to held a more positive thinking. He asked me to remove my labeling to different kinds of experiences life keeps giving to me. So that life became a movie to enjoy other than to judge or to blame on. I forgot to label experiences as good or bad but instead tried to differentiate them as life time experiences helping me to give growth lessons. I chose to live in the moment by keeping my awareness open. Later I decided to place joy and happiness in those moments in order to create peace and harmony. There were many days that I was not feeling whole and happy but I tried to visualize a different story in order to create my own happiness. I tried to search for the feelings and emotions that I hide underneath my actions and worked on them instead of working on others motivations. When I changed my focus on me other than labeling others and situations than my life started to get a better perspective. When my doctor told me to change my focus from labeling to understanding, I became more forgiving, empathic and loving.

I feel lucky that I met these valuable doctors, and had the chance to experience many different kinds of alternative treatments. I am very thankful to my parents that they have supported me to experience them. If I were alone, I would not be able to experience them all as long as they were expensive. However, my parents were understanding to me and wanted me to heal as soon as I could. On the other hand, universe has supported me to find all these wonderful healers. If they were not kind and understanding as they were than I would not be able to continue their practice or dare to experience them. There was always a wonderful vibes coming out of these beautiful people who has helped me to believe in them and also myself.

CHAPTER XVII

October 20th 2013

One year has passed after my surgery. It was my time to have my first yearly check up. So I visited my surgeon in his new office. The hospital was renewed and they have moved to a new building, which was big and modern. I had done all my screenings and tests ready in my hand and was waiting at my doctor's lounge. When my name was called, I felt the excitement within me and walked to his door. When I entered in I was feeling secure.

Dr. Akpinar went through my files before we arrived. So that he had a beautiful wide smile on his face. He told me that I was totally healthy and renewed. It was normal to have some small instability at my heart rates but it would all disappear with time. He said my heart was as healthy as his now. I was very happy. I imagined my new life ahead of me. I felt the relief and bliss going through my veins.

During that one year, I went through different kinds of medicines, therapies and alternative treatments and finally they all paid back. I had a wonderful relaxing summer as well. So all my low vitamin D level went back to normal. The test results were all positive on my vitamin levels. I was feeling lucky, colorful, and also much more lively. The summer has played its magic on me as my doctor recommended. So as he said I felt stronger after the summer vacation. On September I started to paint easily and cheerfully.

I also started to exercise with my personal fitness trainer Tony in September. I felt that I was getting stronger and healthier. He was patiently working on putting my heart rate to normal by giving me less and more exercises under his attendance. I started to control my eating and sleeping habits. I became a brand new person. All my chest pains and depressions have changed into a comfortable peaceful manner. A year later I was able to understand how a healthy body is likely to be. It reflected on my attitude, work and life style. I was feeling much more energetic. All my relationships changed, some friends left me, some came back with apologies, and some got lost. I realized that one-year was meant to be my cleansing time.

I started to pray every night, as I understood the power of prayer during my stay in the hospital. I started to be more grateful and thankful towards life. I was able to breathe in my full potential. Time thought me to be patient. A year and a half later, my heart rate became normal. I was able to exercise in my full potential. I started to spend much more time with my family. Everybody felt to be more tolerable and livelier to me that I understood all was my illusion from my pain in the past. All was past now.

February 6, 2014

The big day has arrived. I started painting on September and the last two paintings finished on the first week of February. They were all gathered together in the gallery space and waiting for the opening on Thursday the 6th of February. I told the gallery on Tuesday that the last two paintings were done so they came to pick them up from my studio. They wrapped them and than carried them to the truck.

After they left, my studio became silent and empty. I looked into the empty room and realized how proud I was with myself. The paintings would be speaking for myself in the next couple of days. I imagined the period of time I worked on them. I started to paint with difficulty of breathing at the beginning but towards the end I was so much better that I got into painting them much more easier than before. I painted everyday for hours that I could not stop. I examined all the heart anatomies, anatomy books and my notes while I was working. I would spread all the books around my studio and look through them and paint. They were telling me what to do and I was following them. Canvas leaded me and insisted me to open up my emotions so did I. I was meditating on them and asking to give me the healing to spread around me.

Now all was out and it was time to show people what I have done. Let my paintings to tell them what I have been through and show them how much I grew up in the last two years. It was time for the paintings to speak to the people who would feel them. I was excited and a bit anxious to see the reactions of people. The gallery owner motivated me and has done a great catalogue. I worked on the catalogues opening page and wrote the exhibitions mission. It all looked wonderful to me as long as it was my first catalogue ever. I looked over the work and I felt like going through my last two years album. Each of them was telling a story of me but also telling the myth of hope.

Opening day

On the opening day all our invited guests arrived. It has been two years since my last exhibition that I have forgotten the feeling of seeing so many people together. I greeted everybody and watched the visitors gathering in front of my works. The paintings, images, colors and every each line were carrying my intense feelings. I was happy that they were all outstanding there for the people to see. Everyone was staring at them and questioning the details. It was as if they were checking on my lines or wrinkles. I was feeling naked but at the same time courageous to be able to let all my emotions out.

It went well. I finally felt that a period of my life has ended that it was time to walk in new chapters of my life. It was difficult for me to be in that crowd as long as I have not been with so many people for the past one year. I was used to my silence and solitude that it was a practice for me to socialize myself as I used to. The experience was all a challenge for me. People questioned the meanings and feelings behind the paintings. It was good that they all saw something different than each other. They said that they felt different during the show.

Some foreign visitors also came to see the exhibition. One lady was from Canada who was very interested in my work. She said she was touched by the details and the meanings that she felt behind the work. She found them to be well thought and put. She gave me her details to stay in touch. It was a great pleasure to meet new people through my work. There were also some Indian visitors who have insisted on me to visit India as long as I was using some Sankrit letters and yoga images. They questioned my interest and knowledge on Hinduism. It was wonderful to meet them and see many different people from various cultures. It was like how I wanted it to be.

Many people from many different religions gathered there. There was a variety standing there to question my idea on oneness of religion. The political situations in my country has made them question the possibility of everyone accepting their variety but gathering together peacefully in oneness. We were there in a country that stands as a bridge between Asia and Anatolia and questioning possibility of everyone accepting their differences with peace was a challenge for everyone.

At the end of the exhibition I was feeling tired but also relieved. Some of the paintings were sold and went to their new houses. I listened to the stories of the buyers and their reasons to be interested with their picks. I wished for my aimed healing to reach at all of the new owners. I healed through my work and wished everyone to be healed with its energy.

Visiting Mother Mary's House

After I was done with my exhibition, I felt like it was time for me to visit Mother Mary's House at Ephesus İzmir, Turkey. I organized the whole trip with a very close friend of mine. We have been talking about visiting Mother Mary, Ephesus and Artemis Temple for a long while. I wanted to sense the wonderful high energy in the place and stay at Şirince town. We thought April would be a wonderful time to sense the spring and the sun, right before Easter.

My wonderful close friend who is from Egypt accompanied me for the visit. We chose the hotel in Şirince through my best friend's advice who has visited the place a year before for a meditation camp. We booked our bungalow houses with the fireplace and arranged a car to take us around with her help. We booked a flight from Istanbul to Izmir and waited for a month with excitement. I was imagining the place and making a nice list for my friend's wishes and mine.

The day came to take our trip and it all went fast and well. The hotels car came and picked us up from the airport and drove us to the town for one hour. We arrived at night that we were not able to see much but there was a great night sky with a bit of rain. The half moon was sneaking at us between the clouds. We arrived at the town and town's dogs greeted us by barking than licking our feet. We went into a small traditional restaurant and served by wonderful town's people who have been smiling all the time. We felt so lucky and peaceful.

Friday morning was our first day to visit all the sights. We got into a mini bus arranged to take us around. We started to drive around green lands under a bright sunny sky. We arrived at our first destination, which was Mother Mary's House. As soon as we arrived at the place we felt peace settling into our hearts. The house was in a wonderful green forest filled with pine cone trees, purple flowers, beautiful roses, and birds that sing all the time. The wind was whispering a romantic peaceful melody. We started to walk through a green path leading us to Mother Mary's House. There were information boards explaining the history and the religious importance. Finally we reached the little stone house with a bronze Mother Mary statue outside. There was a prayer written underneath the statue by Saint Francis from Assisi where is the second location I wanted to visit for a long time.

When we got into the house, we realized the simplicity and also the divinity of the place. We sat at a chair and enjoyed the moment with peace. I prayed and thanked God for giving me the strength to visit God's House. I was grateful to gather my health and strength. I was so happy. I closed my eyes and felt tears building into them. I dreamed of the first day in the hospital. Mother Mary's icon was next to my bed and I was staring at it and praying to be healthy. I wished that day to visit this sight and offer my gratitude. So at that moment I knew I was so lucky to sense life, peace, happiness and only love. I picked a candle from the house, walked outside and lit it to give my prayers. I wished for only love, peace and light for everyone. I hoped for it to reach to every human's heart. I felt lucky to be alive.

The Last Chapter

This is the last chapter of this book. It is also the last chapter of one part of my life. I have a new heart now. It is a new beginning for me. I feel so grateful for all the experiences I have been through. They were filled with pain but as they said no pain no gain. I am grateful for everything God offers me. Either good or bad I am learning from them.

When they ask me what I wish for life. I just don't know. I don't know because I know that I am not the one to know what is best for me. I can know what I wish in general which is peace, love and light but the rest is in the hands of God. I trust that Universe will bring me the best. I trust my heart and thoughts. I know that I learn through my days either they are good or bad. What is important for me is

Let it be, Let God.

I am thankful to all the people, all the angels who lead me on the way. Every person I met on the way carries the face of God. They all tell me something about self. Self is a deep mystery ready to be discovered every day through Nature it opens up.

Right now I am sitting at the garden of the bungalow house in the town of Şirince. I am thankful to Nature to let me finish the last chapter of this part of my life. I feel cleansed and thankful.